Of Cats and Men

Of Cats and Men

Felix Mackay

 BooksUlster

First published in 2017 by Books Ulster

Books Ulster © 2017

The front cover image shows a deceptively cross-looking Trixie in the foreground with Tegan in the background

ISBN 978-1-910375-53-2 (Paperback)

ISBN 978-1-910375-54-9 (Kindle)

*To Min, Magic, Cutie, Sooty,
Trixie and Tegan for bringing
so much pleasure to my life*

Preface

I can understand why many people feel indifferent to cats. In a way, I do too. Other people's cats *generally* do not interest me and I feel no natural inclination to pet or make a fuss over them. Cats do a lot of pottering about, sitting impassively and lying inertly, so to outsiders the desire to have one around the house is understandably a mystery. Unlike most dogs, cat personalities are not immediately obvious. But cats do have characters as unique and diverse as dogs—or humans, for that matter. It is a question of getting close enough to really know them. That is what those who have never shared their lives with a cat fail to realise, and why they find the attachment of others to them so incomprehensible.

Cats are often thought of as detached, cynical exploiters of human beneficence who, through instinct, seek food and shelter from wherever they can find it and form no emotional bonds with their providers. That has certainly not been my experience. They do indeed develop a large degree of independence and often only appear home to be fed, watered, and secure a bed for the night, but is that not essentially what children do too? As for cats being emotionally detached, I know that to be untrue.

I started writing this book as a distraction from the grief of losing a loving and much-loved cat. Originally, I intended it merely as a short tribute to him but, as I wrote, it developed into something more. In order to give background to his story I found myself including autobiographical detail as a matter of course. It is not something that I particularly wanted to do as that was not the purpose of the book, and some of the scenes relate to periods in my life that I'd rather forget. However, if nothing else, they provide context and a form of chronology. I also decided to go back to the beginning of my experiences with cats as I felt somehow that the book would otherwise be incomplete.

This is not a story of high drama. It is an account of ordinary cats, people and their lives, but hopefully there is something to be gained from reading it nonetheless. Sometimes a little insight, a valuable lesson, or even a degree of comfort can be gleaned from another's experiences, however mundane.

I have written under a pseudonym because the book was never intended to be about me, but the names of most of the people mentioned in it are real. Much of the latter part of the text has been typed with the finger of one hand as I constantly had an affectionate cat on my knee who required petting and stroking with the other hand.

The images included of our cats are nothing more than family snaps taken over the years, obviously without a view to publication. The two of my first cat Min as a kitten are of particularly poor quality, but they are effectively all I have of her; and the current cats have largely been exercising a policy of non-co-operation, probably pending the appointment of an agent.

Acknowledgements

The author would like to thank Jeffrey Dudgeon for reading the preliminary chapters of the book and giving constructive feedback. He would also like to express appreciation to Ronnie Hanna for proof reading the text, Laura Vocelle for giving permission to use images from her website (thegreatcat.org), and to Peter Tafuri for providing encouragement.

Contents

Illustrations

Chapter 1

Minette

The first cat I had was forced upon me. I was single and living in a flat in a housing estate on the outskirts of Belfast. On visiting a married couple on the estate, whose cat had just had kittens, I was implored by them to give one a home. There were no pets in our house when I was a boy. My father seemed to have a particular aversion to animals, which I always found strange considering that he was brought up on a farm in a traditional farming family. So the notion of taking a kitten held no appeal for me, especially as I hadn't the faintest idea of how to look after one. Furthermore, at that stage in my life I had no desire for any ties or responsibilities and, even if I had wanted to take on a pet, I certainly wouldn't have chosen a cat. But my hosts were so very insistent and persuasive that I finally relented, with a great deal of reluctance and foreboding.

I kept the kitten for about a week, but found that it was taking up more of my time and attention than I was prepared to give, so I took it back to where it came from before it was too late. They would find another, more suitable home for it I was sure.

It was perhaps another week before I returned to visit that couple again, thinking that the kitten would have probably been rehomed by then. There was no sign of it when I entered their living room but, as soon as I sat down, it appeared from behind the settee and made its way directly to me. Apparently, it had spent most of its time there since I had returned it. Whether that was true or not I will never know, but I didn't have a heart of stone, so that was me trapped.

I brought the tortoiseshell kitten home with me again and we began the process of getting to know each other. I struggled to think of an appropriate name for her, but eventually settled on 'Minette', which is French for 'puss'. For convenience, that later got contracted to 'Min'.

It wasn't too long after her return that a major catastrophe happened. I had left potatoes boiling on the cooker when Min decided to slip through the small gap between the back of the cooker and the wall to investigate what might be there. I cannot remember now what alerted me to the situation—whether she let out a cry of pain, or I heard the electric shock, or smelt the resultant burning—but I rushed into the kitchen, pulled the cooker forward and extricated Min from the internal components. One of her pads was badly burnt and she was completely limp and lifeless. I thought that she was dead until I saw some movement in her eyes. In a panic, I laid her on the hallway carpet and fled out the door, randomly running around the vicinity looking for help. The only responses I got were that she would probably die or that I should get her to a vet. But I was a mature student living off a grant and had no telephone or transport, so getting her to vet wasn't a realistic proposition.

I returned to the flat in a state of despondency and terrible trepidation at what I might find. But no sooner

One of only a couple of just about usable photographs of Min as a kitten. I must have had a cheap camera at the time. This was taken in the days before mobile phones with cameras existed.

The only other surviving and usable picture of Min as a kitten

was I through the door than I saw Min frolicking about as though nothing at all had happened. I need hardly describe my sense of relief. Needless to say too, the first thing I did was to ensure that she could never again get into the back of the old cooker. The claw on her scorched pad remained permanently extended for a while until both toe and claw eventually fell off, but it didn't seem to bother her unduly.

Min, like most kittens, was full of life and mischief, frequently climbing up the blankets that acted as curtains (they were nailed to the wooden battens) or darting about the flat in a mad, senseless frenzy. Rather than being a bind on me, as I had anticipated, she became the reason for me wanting to get home.

I didn't have very much money at the time—nor much since, as it happens—so my diet consisted largely of boiled potatoes, usually supplemented with either peas or some variety of bean. My culinary skills were rather basic too. However, once in a while, I would allow myself a treat, like a bag of crisps (potato 'chips' to any American readers) and quickly discovered that Min had a penchant for them too—cheese and onion flavour being her particular favourite. I suppose she was as bored with her regular regimen of cheap tinned cat meat as I was with boiled potatoes.

The flat (maisonette, actually) was on a second storey beside an incinerator that served the whole block, and I didn't feel comfortable at the thought of exposing Min to the dangers of the environment, so she effectively became a house cat. I did feel sorry for her being confined indoors, but at the time it was safest choice.

Chapter 2

The Bookshop Cat

About three years passed. I got married in the meantime, had a child, but was still living in that same rented maisonette. The flat roof leaked so that a line of receptacles—tins, cups and bottles—had to be placed on the bedroom floor to catch the rain dripping through. The donk-ping-plopping made quite a symphony at times. On one occasion water got into and fused all the electrics but, as we had nowhere else to go, we had to make do as best we could until the council got around to fixing them. The draught through the windows was so bad that it could blow the curtains out by almost 45 degrees when the wind was particularly strong. And as there was no lift, the child's pram had to be hauled up and down a couple of flights of concrete stairs whenever we went out. It was not exactly an ideal family home.

I dropped out of my university course and bought the second-hand book business in Belfast at which I had been on placement. Since I had no capital, it was agreed that I could complete the transaction in monthly instalments over the course of a year. At the end of that period the former owner and I agreed to go into a partnership on the premise that two together could achieve more than each on his own. My family and I, including Min, of course, moved to Bangor, County Down, a seaside town on the shores of Belfast Lough, where I was to run a bookshop. We rented a small terraced house on Gray's Hill, a street that led down to the seafront. It was a rather dilapidated house—I particularly remember the kitchen floor was always covered in a criss-cross of slug trails in the morning and that all we had to cook on was a camping stove—but it was a step up from what we were used to and it had the luxury of a yard-cum-garden. This meant that Min was able to get out properly for the first time, which pleased me no end, and her too, although in the early days there was the worry that she would lose her way home.

In our naivety it didn't dawn on us that she might hook up with a tom cat on her travels, but it soon became apparent that she had. When the time came, Min made her way upstairs to the attic room and was given a box with a blanket in it on which to lie. She gave birth to four kittens but, sadly, only two survived. We found good homes for them in due course.

Our stay in that house was to come to an abrupt end. The landlady came around one day and demanded to have the camping stove as her daughter needed it to heat her dogs' food! That left us with nothing to cook on, of course. She had been happy to have us there at the beginning and her rent money had always been paid on time, so the sudden change in attitude came as a bit of a shock. I heard through the grapevine that she had someone else lined up as a tenant who was willing to pay more rent, so she wanted us out. Even though she was elderly and comfortably wealthy, she was still greedy for that little bit more. I have met quite a few like her in my life and their attitude puzzles me. As the old saying goes, there are no pockets in a shroud.

I suppose I could have invoked all sorts of rights and made a fight of it, but who wants to live under circumstances like that? Thankfully, the bookshop I was running had been relocated from the High Street to Dufferin Avenue shortly before and, by a stroke of good fortune, the two-bedroom flat above it had just become available. So we upped sticks and moved in above the shop.

I cannot recall if Min was ever let out of the building. There was a small yard at the back of the shop, but as we were close to the centre of town, with busy roads around us, it is possible she was kept indoors again. I do remember her sunning herself in the shop window though, much to the amusement of passers-by, especially the children.

As she got older Min got a bit crotchety at times. At nights, she was in the habit of crawling under the bed clothes and tucking herself in behind my legs. If I so much as tried to move a muscle, I would receive a low warning growl, and Min was just as bad.

Our new landlord, Brian Meharg, was amiable and helpful. Although John Neill & Sons acted as his agent, Brian would often pop in personally to see how we were getting on and would occasionally buy a book too. As landlords go, I couldn't have wished for better. Trade in the little second-hand bookshop could be very slow at times, particularly in the winter months, so the struggle for money continued. It being a little off the beaten track didn't help matters either. On one occasion I was late paying the rent and John Neill & Sons, as obliged to do, sent me a rather firm reminder. It wasn't as though I had the money and was deliberately withholding it so, in frustration, I wrote back to say as much. I heard nothing more about the matter and the arrears were paid at the earliest opportunity. Brian never so much as mentioned it to me.

Despite the constant financial battle, I was very happy in that little shop and flat. But circumstances were set to change once more.

Chapter 3

The Great Betrayal

Out of the blue, my business partner, older and supposedly wiser than me, came up with the hare-brained idea of setting up a bookstall in a market along the promenade in Blackpool, England. With the number of visitors there in the summer months, he reasoned, there would be plenty who would want a book to read on the beach or back in their holiday lets in the evening. It was a sure-fire winner and bound to generate untold wealth. I was unconvinced and argued that there were things that we could do to improve the existing business in Bangor first, before venturing into the unknown. I was ignored. Of course, he didn't intend to go himself—that was to be my call of duty. At that point I should have said 'If it's such a good idea, then you do it', but I didn't, and I was ultimately persuaded to be the one to go. I hadn't yet developed the backbone to say 'no' to people. Firmness often only comes with age and through experience. Nor had I lived long enough to appreciate that there is an abundance of people out there who have no idea what they are talking about, but are convinced that they do.

The plan was that I should go in advance to sort out the rental of the stall and organise accommodation. My business partner would come across later in a van with the stock.

Going to Blackpool meant closing the little shop that I loved and uprooting my family again. But the most serious implication, because it was irreversible, was that Min would have to be rehomed. Taking her to England into an uncertain form of rented accommodation, and possibly carting her periodically backwards and forwards across the Irish Sea, wasn't really going to be practicable.

The decision to leave Min behind was the hardest that I had made in my life thus far. It was also the wrong decision, and I have regretted it ever since, but it at least taught me a harsh lesson that meant I was never likely to make the same mistake again.

Through a contact in my son's nursery, a woman was found who was prepared to give Min a home, but only on the condition that we would never ask for her back. Strangely, I don't remember the day I took Min to her new house. What I do recall vividly is returning a day or two later to discover that no one was in. I called to Min through the letter box and saw her bounding down the stairs to the door. Walking away after talking to her for a while was not an easy thing to do.

I'm not sure why I paid that visit. Either it was for a last goodbye or I was suffering a crisis of conscience and might yet have changed my mind. At this distance in time I cannot be sure.

That must have been around April 1989 when Min was about six. It was to be some years before I got to see her again.

Chapter 4

Blackpool

As I had feared, the Blackpool venture proved to be a debacle, a complete and utter fiasco. Despite being in what seemed a reasonable location near the North Pier, the market was often deserted for extended periods of time. Perhaps there were just too many markets and stalls in Blackpool chasing too few customers and their money. During the busy spells it was the long-tried-and-tested stalls that did the business, while book sales were few and far between. I think in the opening weeks I might just have covered the rent with a little to spare, although it's quite possible that the stall was making a loss from the very start. I know that it didn't take too long before I had to start supplementing my income by working for other stallholders who had wares that Blackpool visitors actually wanted to buy.

I minded the watch stall, sold novelty slippers and even manned a fortune-telling machine for a while, although my sales technique on that was found rather wanting. I was casually and politely asking passers-by if they would care to have their fortune told, only to be greeted by a series of head shakes in response. Then an old hand in the world of markets, a Cockney, if I recall correctly, came across and said, 'That's not the way to do it. Watch me.' I stepped aside. 'Here,' he called out to the potential punters, 'come and see this!' and he beckoned them across with his hand.

Surprisingly few ignored him, and once he had them at close quarters he would ask, 'What's your name, sir? And what's your date of birth?' and a couple of other meaningless questions to allow the requisite data to be input into the machine. Then he would press a button, take their cash and hand over a useless piece of paper that no doubt went straight into the nearest bin or got thrown on the ground a few yards further along. But he got their money.

I tried his sales pitch, somewhat half-heartedly, I confess, because it didn't sit easily with me to railroad people into doing what they didn't really want to do. That reticence to be in any way duplicitous was to prove an obstacle to my success in another job that I was to take on very shortly afterwards.

Up to this point I had kept the book stall going. If I was working elsewhere, someone would call me over to deal with the occasional buyer. But it got to the stage where it became pointless to carry on. I made an arrangement with the Pakistani man who owned the watch stall next to me to temporarily set up shop in the front room of his house which was on a street that ran parallel to the promenade. I had brought my car over, so was able to shift the stock in a number of runs in that.

Mr Shah also offered to accommodate me, my wife and my young son at his house. My wife and son had been staying at my father's house while I was trying to establish myself in Blackpool, so this offer came as a godsend and I arranged for them to come over. That was in early July 1989. Mr Shah wasn't a bad sort, I believe, but what we hadn't bargained on was his wife.

What exactly was going on in my head at that time, I have no idea. Where I thought this was all going, I just couldn't say. Why I didn't head straight back to Bangor at this point is a mystery to me now. It would have been the sane and sensible thing to do. Perhaps I didn't want to admit defeat, and pride was driving me to battle on. Whatever the reason, I certainly wasn't thinking straight.

Selling books from the front room of a terraced house was never likely to succeed, even though there was a reasonable footfall past the door; but sometimes, when you are desperate, you clutch at straws. And at least it gave me breathing space to figure out the next move, I suppose.

Meanwhile, Haley, my wife, got a job minding the three children of a couple who ran a food stall in the market. Mr Shah and his Malaysian wife—let's call her 'Lucky'—had a baby daughter who was also unceremoniously dumped on Haley to look after. With our son, that made five young children in her care.

Lucky ran a jewellery stall in another market near the South Pier. Until my wife arrived she had to take her little girl with her. Lucky was mean, bad tempered, thoroughly self-serving and money-driven, with not a charitable bone in her body. In her eyes, other human beings were merely there to be used to meet her own ends, if she could get away with it. She would never have allowed Mr Shah to offer us a helping hand unless there was something in it for her, so my guess is that the baby-sitting service had all been pre-planned.

I paid Mr Shah a nominal rent for the use of the front room, but the accommodation was theoretically free. It consisted of the one upstairs bedroom still intact—the rest of the floor was a derelict building site—with the Shahs living downstairs. My son slept on a single bed and my wife and I had a mattress on the floor. There was a door at the bottom of the stairs that Lucky bolted at night so we were effectively held prisoner—with no toilet or other facilities—until the door was unbolted again in the morning.

The house was Edwardian, I reckon, and the bedroom had a cold, creepiness to it. I remember Haley and I walking into it one night only to discover our son, who was three at the time, sitting bolt upright in his bed. He told us he had been talking to an old man who was standing by the opposite wall. That gave me goose bumps. It could have been a dream, of course, but that's not how it seemed to me.

Mr Shah must have been in his fifties. He was a quiet, unassuming man by nature, with a philosophic outlook on life. He was humorous too, with an innate gift for story telling. I laughed long and hard at his artful depiction of the tigress at Lahore zoo who would deliberately and habitually turn her back on visitors to spray them with pee. Unlike the stereotypical Pakistani businessman, Mr Shah seemed rather disinterested in the acquisition of money. He never ran short of pretexts to abandon his stall and go off on a jaunt. Lucky was much younger than him, in her late twenties. I never thought to ask where they had met, but it couldn't have been a worse match. They had blazing rows. She would fly at him in a rage, shrieking like a banshee, and he would have to physically restrain her. When they married, he thought that he was getting a submissive young wife, and she thought she was getting a successful businessman who would keep her in comfort for the rest of her life. Neither got what they bargained for.

Shah came up with the suggestion that I could make a bit of money by selling leather footballs from the front of the house and he organised a supplier through the Pakistani network. The balls went like hotcakes and I was constantly going back for more. They sold so well, in fact, that the supplier decided to substantially hike up the cost price, and that was the end of that venture.

Meanwhile Haley had got a job working nights in a nursing home, but she continued to look after the children during the day, as well as dealing with the washing, cleaning and ironing that Lucky dumped on her. She grabbed a little sleep whenever she could. I trawled the local paper for a job and got taken on by a double-glazing firm, selling on a commission-only basis. But in order to do well in that line you have to have few scruples. It is all about pressurising and duping people into parting with their money. The ends are thought to justify the means. For instance, one ruse is to tell the potential clients that there is currently another job being done in the vicinity and that if they sign immediately on the dotted line then they can benefit from a huge discount as there would be cost savings from having a team working on two jobs in the same area. It is nonsense, of course. There is no other job in the vicinity, there would be no savings even if there was, and there are no genuine discounts. The reps simply start off with an inflated price and spin a story in order to offer what appear to be generous reductions. People then think they are benefiting from a particularly good deal and will be saving themselves a lot of money. It's all psychological.

When I later visited a great aunt in Cumbria she was singing the praises of the double-glazing company that had recently fitted her new windows. Apparently they had given her a massive discount on the understanding that they could have her old windows. 'But,' she said ponderously, 'they haven't come back to collect them yet.' I tried to explain that the last thing they wanted was her old windows, but she wasn't having any of it. What they had done in effect was to leave her with the bother of dumping them and have her thank them for it.

If someone really wants double-glazed windows and, on the reasonable assumption that there is little material difference between one company's product and another, then there is no real harm done, I suppose. All the reps are doing is employing a degree of deception to ensure that the money comes their way rather than going elsewhere. Still, I was uncomfortable with the sharp practices and decided to play it straight, and that is probably why I didn't have a great deal of success. They say that honesty pays, but one wonders at times.

Haley came back exhausted from a shift at the nursing home one morning. She finished at 8 a.m. and only had a couple of hours before her child-minding duties began. So she went to bed to try to snatch a bit of rest. As she lay there, Lucky came in and dropped her baby beside Haley, saying, 'There's some ironing to do downstairs when you get the time.'

Lucky set off for work. My wife got the baby dressed and wheeled her round to the market.

'Look after your own child!' she said to Lucky, boiling with anger.

'If I do, then I'll have to charge you rent,' was Lucky's reply.

'And you'll have to pay me for washing, cleaning and ironing,' Haley snapped back. And with that, she turned on her heels and marched back to the house.

That was the signal that it was time to leave. Haley had effectively become Lucky's slave.

That evening the nursing home owner was informed that it was my wife's last shift. To his credit, and hers, he offered us accommodation if she would only stay on. But my mind was made up to go. I'd had my fill of Blackpool.

The next morning, when Shah and Lucky (with her baby in tow) had left for work, we packed our bits and pieces into the car, abandoned the books, and flitted to my uncle's place in Appleby, Cumbria.

Chapter 5

Appleby

Uncle Fred was a tall, shy, gentle man. A little bit odd, perhaps, but in a perfectly harmless way. He'd had a tough life. When my grandfather died in an accident in 1933 the family farm in Northumberland had to be given up. My grandmother was left virtually destitute with three young boys to raise, Fred being the eldest and my father the youngest. She took on a series of cleaning jobs and sang and played the banjo in pubs at night to make ends meet. As soon as he was old enough, Fred went out to work as a farm hand to help her support the younger boys. Thanks to him, the younger brothers had the opportunity to get a good education at Appleby Grammar School. The middle one went on to become a successful and wealthy businessman. My father served as a radio officer in the merchant navy and later became the principal of a college for marine radio and electronics. Fred ended his working days, rather ironically, as the groundsman at Appleby Grammar.

When his younger brothers left home and were out fending for themselves, Fred took off to New Zealand for a while to work on a sheep farm. A few years ago, literally on his deathbed, my father told me that Fred suffered an unspeakable experience out there, something so awful that it permanently affected his mind. I was shocked at what I heard, and it made me feel worse than I already did about the way in which I left him.

I wouldn't say that Fred was shunned by the wider family, but perhaps it could be best put that he was accepted under sufferance. If he arrived on a visit nobody would be unkind to him, but they were generally all relieved when he went. He never got married, and spent his adult life entirely alone, apart from the times when he had a dog for a companion.

On the few occasions that I was taken to visit him as a boy, he was living in a squalid bedsit and sleeping on a camp bed. He wasn't a young man anymore, and had been quite badly injured by a kick from a horse, so work was not so easy for him to get as it used to be.

When we arrived on his doorstep he was in much happier circumstances than he had been in previous years. He had his job as groundsman and a nice little newly-built maisonette to live in. It had two bedrooms, a living room and a small kitchen. This was to be our home too for the next few months. Fred gave up the main bedroom for Haley and me. He decorated the small bedroom for our son, who he always called Peter, even though that wasn't his name, and bought him a bed. Fred went back to sleeping on a camp bed in the living room.

For a week or so I continued to work for the double-glazing company, travelling from Cumbria to Lancashire and back every day to meet appointments. But when I found myself falling asleep at the wheel and nearly veering off the road one evening, I decided that it was no longer worth the journey for all that I was earning.

There was an antiques/bric-a-brac shop in Appleby at that time which was run by a friendly couple who also sold books. I asked them if they were interested in buying more stock and they said that they would certainly take a look. So I hired a van and the next morning headed off to Blackpool again.

I timed my arrival in Blackpool to coincide with the Shahs being out at their stalls. I must still have had a key. But when I pulled up outside the house, to my dismay, I saw the front door open and assumed that at least one of them was at home. I had really wanted to avoid the possibility of a confrontation, but I had come this far and I needed those books, so I steeled myself and went in. To my relief, Shah and Lucky were indeed at work. They had rented out the front of the house to someone else in the meantime. The books had been shifted to one of the derelict rooms upstairs. I packed them in boxes, carted them downstairs and loaded them into the van. It must have taken me an hour or two. Fortunately, this was in the days before just about everyone had a mobile phone, otherwise the new tenant might have alerted the Shahs to my raid.

When I started the van engine and pulled off, I mentally punched the air. I had nothing against Mr Shah—in fact, it is quite possible that he was keeping the books safe in the event of my return—but there is no knowing what trouble Lucky might have caused.

The antiques shop in Appleby bought consignments from me over the course of the following month or two. But the supply was obviously finite and I needed to generate a regular source of income. I started touring the wider district in search of book outlets, using my knowledge to buy from one and sell to another at a profit. That could be done in the pre-Internet days. Today anyone can check book prices instantly online but, back then, you either had to have the knowledge or printed reference material to know the market value of a book.

As an example, I remember buying a book illustrated by Hugh Thomson for £5 and showing it to Fred that evening. I told him that I would write to a dealer in Belfast who specialised in that type of book and offer it to him for £25. Fred was entirely sceptical. He looked at me in an almost pitying way. That's not how things worked and nobody would pay that sort of money for a book. When the cheque arrived he was stunned. It was as though nothing in the world made sense anymore. Every penny Fred had earned had been through hard, physical labour, so direct exposure to the concept of such 'easy' money was a revelation to him.

The pickings weren't rich enough in that part of rural England for me to ever make anything more than a bit of pocket money out of buying and reselling books, and job opportunities there were thin on the ground. Haley, however, managed to get work behind the bar in a local hotel so between us we were bringing in enough to get by.

Fred was not the demonstrative type, but it was nevertheless obvious that he enjoyed us being with him. He had been on his own since he was effectively still a boy and now he had a family again. He even mooted the possibility of buying a house. Although his earnings were meagre, he had always lived frugally (apart from the chain-smoking) and had accumulated savings over the years.

Appleby was expanding. Many outsiders had been buying up properties to have as second homes. Housing had become much more expensive and difficult for locals to obtain, so new developments were being built to meet the demand. Fred took us round to see a little red brick bungalow that might serve as a home for us all. But by that time I was thinking of a return to Bangor.

It is not easy to establish yourself without capital in a place where you have no history. Although Fred would have provided us with a home, I couldn't see any prospects for the immediate future other than in a series of soul-destroying menial jobs. Since I first stumbled into it, bookselling was my passion and vocation. Any work I took in the interim was only ever a stop-gap measure until I could find a way back to it. I just didn't have the money or contacts to make setting up a book business in the area very likely any time soon, so I had decided to head back to where I could.

Telling Fred wasn't easy. He sat impassively and didn't say very much, but I'm sure that it hit him hard. I asked him to come to live with us when we were settled again but, to be honest, I didn't really mean it, and was banking on a refusal, which I got. It would never have worked and, at that stage in his life, Fred would have been like a fish out of water in anywhere but his native haunt.

When we left Appleby that was the last time I saw Fred. As far as I recall, I made no contact with him after that. At first I was busy trying to re-establish myself in Bangor and, after that, I suppose I just constantly got caught up in the day-to-day affairs of life. But that is no excuse, and it was unforgivable.

Fred died alone in his maisonette about four years later. It was several days before his body was discovered.

Chapter 6

The Return of the Native

When we left Appleby, in November 1989, we drove to Cairnryan in Scotland and took the ferry across to Larne, on the coast of County Antrim. Then we headed to my father's house which was about 20 miles away. The plan, I think, was to stay there a few days until I could get us fixed up in Bangor again. It didn't work out that way.

My father would have been delighted that the English adventure ended in disaster and that I had to come back with my tail between my legs. Not because he wanted to see me fail, but because he hadn't wanted us to leave in the first place. More particularly, he had wanted his grandson to stay within easy visiting distance. He had developed an attachment to him, which was a good thing in theory, but he was perhaps a little too attached. He always thought he knew what was best for the boy and would meddle at every turn. That, of course, is much better than if he were entirely disinterested, as my surviving grandfather was with me, but it could be extremely exasperating at times.

My father immediately assumed complete control over the boy's welfare and, that night, when our son several times became unsettled in bed, he rushed in to tend to him to the exclusion of all others. A row broke out, I lost my temper and said to Haley, 'Right! Get your things together—we're going!'. Haley, quite rightly, refused to lift our son from bed so late at night and drive off when we had nowhere else to go. At the time, I was furious that she didn't stand shoulder to shoulder with me, no matter what. We were fortunate that my father was there to offer us shelter, but I felt awful about putting us in the position of being obliged to him in the first place. My pride was already wounded enough, so I wasn't going to back down.

I drove off to Bangor on my own and spent the night in the car. As soon as the estate agent's office was open in the morning, I went in and asked 'What rentals do you have with immediate possession?' There was a second storey flat off the Donaghadee Road available and, when I viewed it, I could see why. I imagine that it had been lying empty for quite some time. The lights and the cooker worked, but the wall sockets were essentially useless because they dated back to the 1940s or 50s and were designed for appliances with what were long since obsolete round-pin plugs.

I collected Haley and my son from my father's house and took them back to our new home. Haley was suitably impressed. We had no heat, nothing to plug a heater into, and were back to draughty windows, but at least the roof didn't leak. The first few nights we used whatever clothes we weren't wearing as a mattress. Quickly, however, we got organised and, with a few select purchases from the town's charity (thrift) shops, we somehow made the flat semi-habitable.

Bangor is a seasonal town, although perhaps not so much now as it used to be. Traditionally, before the days of cheap international travel, it was a resort where the well-to-do had holiday homes in which they spent their summers. When I was taken there on day trips or short stays as a boy, it had no end of shops with buckets and spades and plastic footballs hanging outside their doors. There was Barry's amusement arcade, the Tonic cinema, and Pickie Park with its outdoor swimming pool, to name but a few of the attractions. I once won first prize as a scarecrow in a fancy-dress competition at Pickie Park. In later years I told my family that the peculiar thing was that I hadn't even been entered. They reacted much like Queen Victoria—not amused. There was also a joke shop on the High Street which was a veritable Aladdin's cave to me, with its itching powders, X-ray specs, false moustaches, binoculars that blackened your eyes, and lighters that had a snake spring out when you flipped them. We were easily amused back then.

In the winter months Bangor was much less lively and many commercial enterprises would struggle. I remember the High Street in the 1990s being peppered with 'To Let' signs when the summer passed. That doesn't seem to be the case so much anymore, perhaps because the permanent population has greatly increased as Bangor has essentially transformed into a commuter or dormitory town, thus making it able to support more businesses throughout the year.

Whether or not the little shop I had in Dufferin Avenue had been re-let at all in the interim, I couldn't say for sure, but by December 1989 it was vacant again and I reopened there on the 21st. In the meantime, I dissolved the business partnership that I had rashly entered into. It had been a formal partnership, but a loose one to a large degree, in which it was understood that each was primarily responsible for generating his own basic income. Nevertheless, I was still owed something from the business and I took it in stock. I didn't get enough to fill the whole shop, so I bluffed it by putting a lot of the books face out to avoid gaps on the shelves. If anything, that seemed to have a positive effect on sales. The timing couldn't have been more opportune either. People were in a spending mood in the run up to Christmas so I managed to get a nice little turn. I closed on Christmas Day and re-opened on Boxing Day to catch any stragglers who were at a loose end. Every penny counted over that period, as I knew the early months of 1990 would be very slow for trade.

Business was indeed slow and nowhere near enough money was coming in to cover our basic living expenses, so I decided to look for night work. I put an advertisement in the local paper to say that I was available to do relief work for milkmen, covering holidays and days off. I got an instant response and was never short of work after that. Today, of course, that trade is virtually dead. The bottle of milk on the doorstep in the morning is a thing of the past. That saddens me. There was something rather comforting in hearing the clink of bottles being delivered in the early hours; and gone is that tasty plug of cream that one used to get at the top of a bottle of whole milk.

People probably don't realise how tough the milkmen had it. They were out all night, six or seven days a week, running about in all sorts of weather—through ice, snow and storms at times—and had to devote a couple of evenings a week to collecting money from their customers too. It was often not easy for them to get sleep during the day because of phone calls from customers, family commitments, or other affairs that needed attended to in daytime. But the milk had to be delivered no matter what, so they periodically went out half-exhausted, or even ill. I once contracted viral pneumonia when covering a milkman for his holiday, but had to carry on for another three nights, roughly eight hours a night in the middle of winter, until I was able to find another relief worker to take over. By the time the pneumonia had finished with me, I was a bag of bones. I obviously survived and recovered in due course, but not before another milkman rang to ask if I was ready to come back to work, with the encouraging words, 'The exercise will do you good.'

I should say a few words about the milkmen's helpers too. These were generally young lads of school age who wanted to earn a bit of pocket money, and I had a great deal of respect and admiration for them. They had the discipline to get out of their beds at an ungodly hour and run steadily, whatever the weather, often for as little as £5 a night. They knew their 'calls' by heart (the milkmen would tell them of any changes) and on good, dry nights would stand on the van tail bar and fill a crate with customer orders, adding a few bottles in case anyone left a note for extra. When the first call in the sequence approached, the milkmen would slow down, allowing the boys to jump off, crates in hand, and go about their deliveries. The milkmen would drive forward to the next cluster of calls. It was all timed to perfection so that the helpers would catch up just as the milkmen were finishing their own batch of deliveries. Then off they would go again.

I didn't think about it at the time—I just took things as they were—but it's a wonder that the child protection and health and safety agencies weren't all over it. Perhaps because they were always tucked up cosily in their beds, blissfully unaware of the practice. We all fell once in a while, usually tripping over something in the dark, and maybe sustained a cut or two from broken glass, but I never saw or heard of anyone getting badly injured. Theoretically, and in hindsight, I suppose a case could be made that these boys were being exploited, being put in harm's way, and that their education was likely to suffer, but in practice I believe that the experience was probably more beneficial than harmful to them. I feel that, if anything, it taught them valuable self-discipline and endurance that would stand to their good in the long-term. That certainly seemed to be the case for those I kept in touch with or heard about later.

What killed the trade was cheap milk sold in supermarkets. Most of the milkmen were franchisees of the dairies and those same dairies started supplying the supermarkets at a more competitive rate, thus cutting the throats of their own franchisees. The milkmen were naturally not one bit happy about the situation, and there was a lot of fighting talk at the time, but ultimately it was a battle that they could not and did not win.

In March of 1990 the flat above the shop became vacant again, so we returned to it. We were now back to where we started from, where we had been happy, only this time without Min.

Chapter 7

The Inter-Cat Years

B efore I get back to the subject that I set out to write about—cats—there are a few catless years that I would like to cover for the sake of completeness, if nothing else. I suppose that the cats' lives were so interwoven with ours that taken in isolation they might have less meaning anyway. I will work my way back to Min and on to the other cats in due course, and in as succinct a manner as possible, so bear with me.

Working most nights and then going in a couple of hours later to mind the shop meant that I was often very tired during the day—so tired at times, in fact, that I not infrequently fell asleep. I remember waking up once to the tail end of one of my snores, with my face flat against the desk that I used as a counter, only to see a little pile of coins heaped up in front of me. The bookshop had become self-service.

Life was still tough financially, because the shop could go days without a single sale during the winter and the work on the milk rounds was not particularly well paid, but we managed to muddle along and pay our way. In early 1991, a little two-bedroomed terraced house in Railwayview Street, just across the road from the shop, came up for sale, so we decided to go for it. We had no savings, but this was in the days of 100% mortgages and the repayments worked out at less than the rent we were currently having to pay for the flat above the shop. Finally, we had secured a home of our own and we were euphoric.

In the autumn, our son started school, so that freed Haley up to go out to work too. She was never short of it, because she was always a hard worker. Adequate income was now coming in to keep us ticking over and the little house was cosy and warm. The street was largely populated with families and long-term residents, and the neighbours were friendly and pleasant. We couldn't have wished for more. But the idyll was not destined to last.

On 7 March, 1993, the IRA detonated a no-warning car bomb at the top of Main Street in Bangor which injured four police officers and damaged churches and shops. It went off in the early hours of a Sunday morning when I was sleeping before going out to cover a milk round. I distinctly remember waking up, in a state of utter confusion, to see and feel the bedroom shaking, and thinking that whatever was happening, my life was about to end. But the vibrations gradually subsided and I heard building alarms going off around town. I understood then what had happened.

I jumped out of bed, got dressed, and made my way to the bookshop. Its large, plate-glass window had been blown in. I stood in front of the shop for a while pondering what I could do, but there was nothing that could be done for the moment. Then I walked up the road to look at the destruction done to Main Street. It was appalling, and I thought to myself, 'What is this supposed to achieve? What's the point?'

Railwayview Street from the top

The shop in Dufferin Avenue (the shutterless one with the door) is now a barber's

I returned to the house and got ready to go out again. The milk still had to be delivered. Sundays were generally easier for me as most milkmen 'doubled-up' many of their calls on the previous morning. In other words, on Saturdays they left milk for Sunday as well. This afforded me a lie in until 4 or 5 am as there were fewer deliveries to be made. On the morning of the bomb I collected Steven Dunlop, my regular weekend helper, as usual. Steven never let me down. He must have been 14 or 15 years old when he first turned up at my doorstep, with his friend Paul, looking for work. It was the start of a friendship that to date has lasted 25 years. Steven, as proof of what I said earlier, combined working most nights as a helper on milk rounds with studying to become a mechanic. Today he runs his own car repair business, employing four or five others.

When I got home I discovered that the blast had caused a delayed collapse of the bedroom ceiling and one side of Haley's face had been badly cut by falling plaster. Haley tended to, I went back to the shop to survey the damage in daylight. Glass littered the carpet and small fragments were embedded in most of the books. I cleaned up as best I could and organised getting a replacement window. This wasn't the first time that I'd been close to an IRA bomb. On my way home from school in the 1970s one had been detonated near the centre of Belfast, blowing women and children around me to the ground. This sort of nonsense had been going on since I was a young boy and all our lives were blighted by it to a greater or lesser degree, mine to a much lesser degree than many others who were maimed, seriously injured or who had lost loved ones. But the cost and inconvenience of getting the bookshop open again was a turning point in my life nonetheless. I decided that when the yearly lease was up I would not renew it. Instead, I would work from home and sell books by catalogue, supplementing that income with what I earned from the milk.

The Bangor bomb was only a minor irritation to our domestic tranquillity, however. Our home life was to be shattered by a different, more persistent form of human folly.

Chapter 8

Living Hell

When we moved into our first little home the house next door was vacant and remained that way for a good year or more. Then a local businessman bought the property as a 'buy to let'. The tenants he put in were a man in his mid-forties and a woman in her sixties. Not a bad age group to ensure continued peace and quiet, one would have thought. It didn't turn out that way. Margaret would have been completely harmless by herself. She was a frumpy little grey-haired woman and—there's no other way to put this—perfectly simple. Robert was lacking in the brain department too. You could almost tell just by looking at him that something wasn't quite right, and a short conversation would be enough to confirm it. But he had a low cunning that allowed him to control and manipulate poor Margaret. She was his meal ticket. He was on state benefits and without Margaret's contribution he would have been stuck in bedsit land. A house in a regular residential area suited his purposes better.

Once he was established at his new address, it didn't take him long to seek out groups of young teenagers who were looking for an underage drinking den. I'm sure they thought they'd hit the jackpot, with an adult on call to buy them alcohol whenever they wished, a nice, cosy house to drink themselves silly in, and license to behave in whatever way they pleased—a much better proposition than hanging about the streets or in a cold park where they might attract attention and get moved on.

At first, not knowing exactly what was happening, I let the house 'parties' ride, despite the fact that the music was played so loudly that the walls literally vibrated. I got little enough opportunity to sleep as it was and this almost nightly racket wasn't helping, but I was working on the theory that things would settle down eventually and all would be well again. I was wrong. After several weeks of it, I decided to take action. Realising that it was pointless trying to reason with someone who was evidently non compos mentis, I bypassed Robert altogether. His landlord operated a business from the same street that my shop was on, so I went in to see him and explained the situation. Having heard me out, this pillar of the community and stalwart of the church responded by saying, 'I'm in business to make money.' When I later bumped into Beverley, the young woman who lived on the other side of Robert and Margaret, she told me that she had previously taken the same action and had got the same response. So, that avenue of recourse was closed.

Robert inhabited a seedy world of drinking and gambling. When his benefit money came in it was immediately spent on cigarettes, alcohol and bets on horses, and then he would beg, borrow or steal to keep his habits fed. When Margaret received her pension or benefit payments he would quickly deprive her of those and on more than one occasion I heard her pleading, 'Robert! Robert! Don't take my money!', only the way she pronounced his name it sounded more like 'Rabbit'. Beverley, being at work during the day, was regularly having parcels stolen from her front doorstep. Someone was presumably flogging the contents in pubs around the town to generate some ready cash. Was it the same person taking clothes from her washing line? We will never know. If only Robert had been more vigilant then perhaps he could have caught the culprit red-handed.

The teenage drinking binges continued on a regular basis and the noise made life intolerable for us. There was no escaping from it. Only those who have been through similar experiences can truly appreciate how soul-destroying it is to have no peace in your own home. Whenever I ran out of patience and called the police they would invariably arrive with car sirens blaring and lights flashing, giving the revellers next door ample warning to make their exit through the back and into the alley. I did explain this ruse in my calls, but it made no difference. On a particularly rowdy occasion the police hadn't shown up after over an hour, so I called back. I was asked, 'Oh, so you still want us to come?' 'Well, yes,' I replied, 'if it's not too much trouble.' The station would scarcely have been a one-minute drive away.

From somewhere, for some reason, Robert acquired a dog. For several days, I could hear it howling in his yard, neglected and probably starving. When he did go out to it he abused the dog for making a noise. I rang the USPCA (Ulster Society for the Prevention of Cruelty to Animals). To its credit, the organisation acted swiftly and sent officers almost immediately. I don't know what transpired on their visit, but not long afterwards the dog was gone. A few days later I got talking to a long-term resident of the street who had the colourful name of Trixie Blue. She had evidently had words with Robert about his treatment of the dog because she told me how he had come hammering at her door, accusing her of having called the USPCA. Trixie was in her sixties, living with her adopted daughter, and the experience had obviously unnerved her. 'But I didn't do it,' she said. 'I know you didn't,' I replied, 'because I did—and you can tell him that.' She did, because that evening there was a hammering on our door. Robert didn't have the guts to confront me himself, so he sent one of his low-life drinking pals who was renting another house at the bottom of the street. This nasty little bald-headed man proceeded to threaten to have me 'sorted out' by a local paramilitary group. 'Knock yourself out, kid,' I responded, 'you know where I live. But why don't you go get your buddy and the three of us can sort this out like men? On second thoughts, though,' I added, 'those odds wouldn't be fair on you.' I heard no more about it.

One night I was woken by yelling from the street below. A young man was shouting, 'You raped my girlfriend!' while simultaneously trying to kick Robert's door open. My first instinct was to go and intervene, but I stopped myself, thinking 'No, let nature take its course.' If it escalated, I thought, then perhaps something would finally be done about this menace. I heard the door crash open, then all was silent. Robert, if he was in, had obviously escaped through the back. Margaret was probably in hiding. To my knowledge, nothing came of the incident. My hope of salvation was doomed to disappointment. Robert wasn't carted off in the back of a police van. He simply laid low for a while then it was back to business as usual.

Not long afterwards, I returned from work to see a 'For Sale' sign on Beverley's house. After perhaps a year, the poor girl had come to the end of her tether with it all. I understood perfectly. I wouldn't regard myself, and nor would others, as a shrinking violet or of a particularly nervous disposition, but it had reached the stage where I was living in a state of tension and jumping at the slightest noise. I despised Robert so much for it that I found myself lying in bed at nights fantasising about beating him to pulp. But I knew that it couldn't be done. I would be the one to end up in the dock and have the book thrown at me.

What really took the biscuit was when a knock came to the door on another evening and I opened it to see Margaret standing there.

'Rabbit says will ye borrow him a tenner?' she said.

I was momentarily dumbfounded.

'You can tell Rabbit, "No".'

She stared back at me with that comically gormless expression of hers. It didn't help that she was boss-eyed.

'Why not?'

Poor Margaret. She genuinely didn't understand why there might be a problem. I didn't respond, but started closing the door very, very slowly for a sardonically dramatic effect. Margaret remained motionless, like an immoveable object, staring vacantly all the while. For all I know, she could have still been there an hour later.

Nightmare neighbours though Margaret and Robert were, they did provide the occasional moment of light relief. When Haley and I were treated to an insight into the mating habits of the Rabbit, thanks to thin walls and a running commentary by Margaret, we nearly went into hysterics. 'Is it in yet, Rabbit? Is it in?' If we hadn't been laughing so hard we would have shuddered.

A rumour came to my attention that Robert had been offering money to young girls in the street to show him their knickers. Shortly afterwards, another rumour circulated that he been badly beaten by a group of men and then thrown down the railway embankment. When I saw him a few days later his whole face was badly cut and bruised and I couldn't help but feel elated. However, creatures like Robert never learn. He was subdued and stayed quiet for a while before reverting to all his anti-social ways again. How long can this carry on, I wondered. What next?

Somebody finally did take notice. Out of the blue, we received a visit from the council official in charge of issues relating to nuisance neighbours, although I can't recall the title of the department as it was then. He explained that Robert had been to see him to deny what we had been telling the council. 'It's the first time I've had anyone turn themselves in,' he said, with some amusement. He knew, as we did, that no complaint had been lodged. I hadn't even thought of that possibility. This man recognised immediately that everything Robert was denying was in all probability true and he had the decency to go out of his way to offer help to the victims. He was extremely sympathetic and told us what we had to do to have action instigated, which included keeping a written record of each incident. However, to my recollection, the bottom line was that the whole process could drag on interminably with no guaranteed eviction. We might have to suffer this abuse for years to come. So, like Beverley, we decided to sell up and go. Robert had succeeded in driving us all from our homes.

We sold our little house for a nominal profit. Unfortunately for us, the prices in the street, being close to the town centre, more than doubled in a boom over the succeeding months. We had badly lost out, but at least we were free from mental torture. I did have a conscience about passing on the problem to someone else, and I like to think that I would have ultimately confessed under different circumstances, but my guilt was somewhat assuaged because although it was technically a young woman purchasing the property, her boyfriend seemed to be the one who was instrumental in the deal. Having met him, I felt confident that he would have fewer scruples than I in dealing with Robert. I was sure that Robert would now be made to pay dearly for any misdemeanours.

It was more than 20 years before I felt able to look at that house in Railwayview Street again. I have only recently driven past it. Who knows what became of Margaret. I never heard about her again. But it wasn't the last I was to hear of Robert. About six years later, in April, 2001, I was watching the news on television when a report came on of a man being charged with the attempted abduction of a child from a department store in Bangor. Yes, it was my old chum Rabbit.

Chapter 9

A Fresh Start

Having left Railwayview Street, we rented a detached house on the Clifton Road while we searched for another property to buy. Six months later we were still looking. Perhaps we were being extra cautious after what we had just gone through, but nothing that we felt suitable came to our attention. Detached was obviously our preference, but we knew that financially it could stretch us to the limit. Then Bill Wylie, a milkman for whom I worked periodically, tipped me off about a bungalow for sale on his round. The area, on the periphery of the town, wasn't really my cup of tea, it being a 1960s red-brick development. I preferred Victorian or Edwardian houses, but I decided to have a look anyway, if only out of politeness. It was detached, had a good front garden and a garage, and it was going for a relative song. As it was vacant, I took a walk around the back. That sold it to me. The back garden was sizeable, with lovely flower beds, a pond, and a little green shed.

There was a short bidding war for the bungalow, but we managed to secure it at a price that I felt was still very good value, and affordable to us. When it came to moving in, I borrowed an open-backed milk van to transport the furniture and all our worldly possessions. I'm sure that the new neighbours must have thought the hillbillies were coming. That was in the autumn of 1995.

Financially, things were going quite well for us at the time. The Internet was just beginning to build up steam and I was among the first wave of booksellers online. That period, before seemingly limitless competition started sweeping in, was the most comfortable we had been either before or since. Money was coming in without too much of a struggle, although it still required a lot of hard work to make it, and we had a nice house with a lovely garden. It was at that point that my thoughts turned back to Min. She would enjoy living here. Ignoring my promise never to ask for her back, I got Haley to arrange a visit. It was in my head to offer money for Min. The lady I had left her with, whose name I sadly can't recall, graciously agreed to a visit. When we arrived, I could tell that she felt ill at ease, as though she sensed my intention. She told us that from the outset, whenever her husband made his way upstairs to bed, Min would pounce and attack him. It did cross my mind that my desertion might have been responsible for that. Min was out at the time, but came wandering in later and plonked herself in front of the hearth in the living room, opposite to where I sat on the settee. The lady's grandchildren played around Min, but knew well not to disturb the queen of the house. Min must have been around 12 years old by that time and it had been a long time since I had seen her, but when I called 'Min, Min, Min!' as I used to do, her ears pricked up in instant recognition and she came to me. I have no doubt that she remembered. I petted and stroked her. The lady said, 'She'll let you know when she's had enough.' She was right. After a while Min gave me a warning bite to let me know that my time was up.

It was quite apparent that Min was perfectly content where she was, and much loved too, so I thought better of asking for her back in the end. I left feeling unexpectedly happy and satisfied. Min died about six years later at the ripe old age of 18.

Our new house was in a quiet neighbourhood with plenty of green space around and little traffic on the road. It was ideal for a cat, so I kept my eyes on the local newspapers and eventually spotted an advertisement seeking good homes for kittens. Haley, my son and I drove to a farm about 15 miles away to have a look. The farmer's daughter seemed to have charge of homing the litter and we chatted to her for a while in the kitchen. I don't remember ever getting to see the others because, as I stood there, one adventurous kitten starting climbing up my trouser leg (from the outside, thankfully). He was so full of life and mischief that he couldn't be resisted.

'I think the decision has been made for us,' I said.

The farmer's daughter then pointed to below a radiator from where another kitten was cautiously watching the proceedings.

'She's his little friend. They play and sleep together.'

I gave her a wry smile.

'Okay, okay,' I said. 'We'll take both.'

We drove back to Bangor with the black and white kittens nestled on a blanket in a cardboard box. Not for the last time, we went out for one cat and came home with two.

Chapter 10

Magic and Cutie

As the result of years on night shifts and irregular sleeping hours (although my snoring may have been a contributing factor too), I had my own bedroom. That first night the kittens slept in their cardboard box which I placed on the floor beside the bottom of my bed. As I lay half asleep, through the duvet I felt the pressure of tiny paws making their way along the length of my body. The journey ended at my earlobe, which then got nibbled and licked. That was Cutie, and she did it for the rest of her life. She was still very young and tiny when we got her, so I guess that my earlobe was at first used as a substitute teat for suckling and that the habit just continued.

The other kitten, the leg climber, we called Magic because his tail was black with a little white tip on the end, like a magic wand. Cutie was named simply because she was so darned cute.

They were both rather unwell in the early days, constantly sneezing and leaving strings of gooey snot on the windows. I worried that they had flu. We took them to the Glenn Veterinary Clinic on Bingham Street in Bangor. Linda Glenn was marvellous, and I immediately felt at ease with her. What her actual diagnosis was for Magic and Cutie I can't recall but, after a course of treatment, the sneezing and other symptoms disappeared and the cats began to thrive.

As it turned out, Magic and Cutie did indeed have a bond. Despite being the tom, Magic was always smaller than Cutie and he never grew very big at all. He was a bit of a weakling and tended to hang on to Cutie's metaphorical coat tails. When they had been out on a sortie together, Cutie invariably arrived back first with Magic a second or two behind her. If Cutie caught a mouse, Magic would hover about the action as if to say 'I helped too.' And the day Cutie came through the living room window with a baby's head in her mouth, Magic was right on her tail. I walked in at that very moment and froze on the spot in horror. It took me a split second to process that it was only a child's doll, but life-size and very realistic. She was carrying it by the hair with her teeth.

Magic's appetite was out of all proportion to his size. Cutie was indifferent to food and would eat as and when, but Magic was always on the scrounge. Nothing could be left safely on the kitchen surfaces and, at mealtimes, if it was something to his liking, he would guilt trip me into giving half of mine away. Every movement of the fork from plate to mouth was followed intently and with a look of expectation on his little face. I would start off by saying firmly, 'No, not for you,' but I always cracked in the end. One abiding memory I have of him is of Christmas Days. He sat sentinel for hours by the oven as the turkey cooked. Nothing, but nothing, could entice him away.

His hunting ambitions were disproportionate to his size too. Many times I watched him on the roof creeping up on a gull. I would yell at him to give it up, not so much to rescue the bird, but more to save him from getting a

The author in his role as a bed for Magic and Cutie (foreground)

The author with the ear-nibbling Cutie

pasting. He wasn't built for fighting. Time and again we saw him bolting back to the safety of the house with another cat in hot pursuit. When Haley or I went out to see the other cat off, Magic would spot it in flight and reverse the chase, then halt abruptly at the edge of the garden as if to say, 'Yeah, and don't come back!'

During their first summer with us both Magic and Cutie started coming back to the house with swollen faces. I was incensed. Some cat-hater with a manicured garden was obviously repaying their friendliness by hitting or kicking them. I swore that if I ever found out who it was I'd give them a taste of their own medicine. The one thing that puzzled me was why Magic and Cutie kept going back for more. The swelling would go down and then a few days later their faces were swollen again. Why, oh, why did they not learn their lesson and stay clear? It wasn't until the following summer, when I was sitting on the patio steps enjoying the sunshine, that I saw them having great fun catching bees in their mouths. 'Stupid cats!'

Magic was democratic with his affection and bonded with Haley and me equally. In August 1998, our second son was born and Magic would accompany Haley as she pushed the pram around the neighbourhood. He would often follow her quite some distance from the vicinity of our house. On several occasions in the early years both cats went missing for a day or two, presumably having got shut in somewhere as a result of their curiosity. On one occasion, Magic came back after a couple of days covered in coal dust, having obviously been trapped in somebody's bunker. On another occasion, Cutie went missing and

Haley began door-to-door enquiries, with Magic pottering along beside her. She knocked on one door and said to the lady who answered, 'I'm looking for a black and white cat.' The woman looked from Haley to Magic, who was sitting on the step beside her, then back at Haley again, as if to say, 'Is this a wind up?' Cutie wasn't found, and when she still hadn't shown up after another day or so, I started ringing round local veterinary practices and animal sanctuaries, but to no avail. I remember one woman asking if there were foxes in our area and saying, rather insensitively, 'Because, if so, one of those might have got her.' Foxes did very occasionally stray into our garden and I was truly devastated at the thought of her having met that fate. But, after three long weeks, when all hope had gone, she suddenly appeared at the living room window, looking none the worse for wear.

Naturally, a great fuss was made of Cutie on her return. Goodness knows where she had been all that time. I have a theory that she jumped on to a delivery van and had ended up miles away, then somehow eventually found her way home again. Whatever happened, it was destined to remain one of those frustrating missing cat mysteries.

The next drama was when Cutie injured her back leg. Taking her to the vet was never any fun. Whereas Min had been happy to sit free in the back of the car and look out of the windows, Cutie had to be put in a carrier and she wailed the whole journey. And when I say 'wailed', I mean *wailed*. The more I tried to comfort her, the louder she got. My stress levels went into orbit. She had to have the leg bandaged—I'll never forget that pink dressing—and she was to be prevented from climbing and jumping for several weeks, I think. No climbing or jumping! There was only one way that could be done. I had to build her a pen in the garage, made from bits and pieces of wood and wire mesh that were lying about the premises. It meant constant visits to her throughout the day and night, and climbing in with her so that she could lie with me for a while. When freedom finally came, it is hard to say which of us was the more relieved.

In his fourth year, Magic got sick. He lost his trademark appetite, became lethargic, and just wanted to lie on us for comfort all the time. He started involuntarily peeing in the house too. In ignorance and innocence, we took him to the vet to have him treated and made better. When Linda said that he had cancer I felt as though I'd been hit by a thunderbolt. 'There must be something you can do?' I asked desperately. 'I don't care what it costs.' But there was nothing to be done. Haley and I both went into the treatment room when the time came, but I couldn't stay. I said my goodbyes and left. I have never been able to stay to the very end.

Magic's death really hit me hard. I cried uncontrollably for the first time in my life. For days, I would start sobbing whenever I thought of him. He was such a little character. It would be another 17 years before I cried that way again. I was also very worried about the effect his loss might have on Cutie. She was never lively and full of mischief like Magic, whose tail was always erect like an aerial, so it was difficult to gauge if she was more subdued than normal. Nevertheless, I gave her plenty of love and attention for reassurance sake.

The rest of Cutie's life was largely uneventful. She no longer wandered too far away, but stayed close to home and protected her territory. Neither cat nor dog fazed her. If they strayed on to our property she never hesitated to see them off. When a spaniel got loose in our front garden I ran out to save Cutie, but she went at him like a bat out of hell before I had a chance to intervene. Then a woman with a lead in her hand appeared on the other side of the garden wall. She was in a bit of a flap.

'Have you seen a dog running about?' she asked.

'Yes,' I replied proudly, 'our cat has just chased him through the hedge.

She gave me a look that seemed to combine doubt with indignation, and then walked off.

Cutie never got sick; she just got old. Towards the end there were several times when she was cold to the touch and I had great difficulty rousing her from sleep. I believe that she could have quite easily gone on any of those occasions, but had fought her way back. When I knew the end had finally come, we took her to Linda. As with Magic, I couldn't bear to watch Cutie die, so I said my goodbyes and left the room. Haley stayed with her in her last moments. That was in March 2009 when Cutie was 14.

From the very start, Cutie had gravitated towards me. She was *my* girl. I cleaned her bottom when she was a tiny kitten. She lay on the couch with me in the evenings and slept with me at night. In perfect trust, she would rest on my shoulders as I walked about the house. But when she was gone I didn't grieve for her as I had for Magic. I was sad, of course, but I didn't cry at all. That surprised me, and I felt guilty. Perhaps it was because her death had been anticipated for quite some time and, when it eventually did happen, there was an element of relief. I just don't know.

Chapter 11

Sooty

This is where I come to the cat for whom I started writing the book. Now, this may not be the greatest advertisement for a chapter, but his life was largely uneventful. What follows is more a study in character and a word or two about grief.

Sooty first made an appearance in the final months of Cutie's life. I was sitting on the patio steps, as was my habit, when I saw a black and white cat walk around the corner of the house. He (as I later discovered) was a big boy with a thick bushy tail, but his head seemed disproportionately small to his body. His mouth miaowed as he approached, but not even an audible squeak could be heard. He exercised no caution whatsoever, but immediately came to me to get petted, and I duly obliged. I was struck by his innocent friendliness but, after we parted, I thought no more of him.

A couple of mornings later, when it was still dark, I saw what I thought was Cutie's face at the kitchen door. As I went to let her back in, another face appeared which, through the patterned glass, looked identical. I opened the door and Cutie and the other cat leapt in almost simultaneously. The second cat was the one that had come to me two days before. Cutie turned and hissed at him, but he didn't react at all. The poor thing just looked at me plaintively, but I had to chase him out. My heart wanted to let him in but, for once, my head said 'No.' This had long been exclusively Cutie's home and I didn't want her to feel in any way threatened at her age.

Seen close up it was easy to tell the two apart, but they did have very similar markings. Both were mostly black on top, with a part white face and white chest, underbelly and legs. But, no, Cutie had been spayed long ago and never had kittens.

From that time the other cat seemed to be constantly around and we began to feed him, but always outside. He would appear at the kitchen window, stare in and appeal to us with silent miaows. His white breast was often soiled with coal dust, so we guessed that he was sheltering in our concrete bunker. Hence, we referred to him, rather unimaginatively, as 'Sooty'. It became clear that he had no home of his own and was living rough. This was a source of puzzlement to us because he was such a friendly, good-natured soul who seemed to be used to human company. He certainly didn't come across as a feral cat. We speculated that his 'owner', for want of a better term, had died and that nobody was on hand to look after him. Years later, a volunteer at an animal sanctuary told me that it wasn't unheard of for people to move house and just leave their cats behind. That possibility had not even entered my head. I could never have imagined such cold callousness, although it ought not to have surprised me. If I had the opportunity to have one of life's mysteries revealed to me, above all it would be to know Sooty's history before he came to us.

One cold night, not long after Cutie died, we had lit the fire in the living room and brought a mattress in to lie on so that we could watch television in comfort and warmth. Having gone into the kitchen for a drink, I saw Sooty at the window and opened the door to let him in. Then I returned to the living room and got back under the duvet, leaving the door ajar. Shortly afterwards Sooty made his way in too and proceeded to lie at the end of the makeshift bed. We were quiet and made no sudden movements so as not to startle him. That was his first step in moving into the house.

Over time, as he got to know the layout of the bungalow, us and our routines, he gradually became very settled and comfortable. He would generally be out most of the night and come in during the day to sleep, and he randomly changed which room to rest in and on what. It could be the settee for weeks on end, then suddenly change to a bed for a while. What the deciding factors were, is anybody's guess. But for a long, long time, he very much kept to himself. He was happy enough to be stroked and petted as he lay, but he didn't come to us. It literally took years before he would jump up and lie with me on the settee or on my bed, but, right to the very end, if I so much as moved a muscle, he would jump off again and find another spot to sleep in. In the winter months, he sometimes stayed in much of the night and would lie on my bed until I just had to move, then he might hop onto the padded swivel chair beside it.

For the most part, though, he was out at night, doing whatever it is that cats do. He would periodically arrive

Sooty was a big boy with a big heart. When on my lap it wouldn't take long before my backside went numb, and with those big paws and sharp claws his kneading required superhuman endurance to bear.

Sooty's drinking bowl

back in the morning with cuts and scratches on his nose and, over the course of time, more and more chunks of his ear went missing. Countless times I was woken by the noise of a cat fight outside and had to leap out of bed. Standing outside in my bare feet in the middle of winter and trying to get Sooty into safety was a duty that I could easily have forgone. Sometimes his wounds were more serious, but Haley bathed them and applied antiseptic cream. Unlike many cats, Sooty did not resist treatment. Although in the early days he preferred not to be handled at all, gradually he came to accept being lifted and hugged. My younger son, who grew up with Sooty, loved him to bits. Perhaps, before he was older and wiser, a bit too much at times. On a couple of occasions Sooty was maybe loved to the point of torture, and he struck out for freedom. But I knew Sooty. He may have battled with other cats over his territory, but there wasn't a vicious bone in his body. If he swiped at my son it would have been in desperation and not intended to hurt. Not once in all the years he was with us did he ever show the slightest sign of temper or irritability to me. He was a big, soft, loveable lump whose trademark sign of affection was to butt heads with us.

Sooty was certainly the dopiest cat we'd had. He was never able to associate his appearance at my bed-room-cum-office window with me leaving the room to let him in. Time and again I would return from the front or back door to see him still staring imploringly through the window. When I beckoned him furiously with my arm he simply looked at me in bewilderment. Neither did he ever figure out how (or perhaps he was too lazy) to open a door that was slightly ajar. That was another duty that had to be performed for him. And when it came to catching mice in the house, he was more of a hindrance than a help. Whenever we knew there was a mouse in a room we used to bring Cutie in to flush it out, with Magic there for moral support. She was relentless in her pursuit. The mouse would be caught, retrieved and delivered to safety outside. Sooty, however, was entirely disinterested, even if he heard the mouse scratching about. He would head straight for the door to be let out. Once, when we saw a mouse scurry behind the fridge in the kitchen, we brought Sooty in so that he could pounce when we forced it into the open. He sat impassively, turning his head to watch disinterestedly as it scurried past him. Then he began giving himself a good clean.

I didn't witness it myself, but my wife and son claim to have seen him eating a mouse outside. He certainly didn't bother the birds. They could virtually sit on his head and he'd take no notice. Who knows what went on inside his mind.

There was essentially only a first and last visit to the vet for Sooty. He hadn't been with us too long when Haley and my son came in a panic to tell me that Sooty had swallowed a thin necklace he'd been playing with. I was sceptical. If he had, then he wasn't showing any signs of distress. They hadn't actually *seen* him swallow it, but they were adamant that he had because it had completely vanished without trace. What could I do? I couldn't afford to take the risk, so off to Linda's he went. After examination and X-ray, there was no sign of any necklace in his digestive

Sooty in bed after a hard night's work

'He's behind you!'

system, so home again we came, with me a bit lighter in the pocket. We were not two minutes through the door when I heard Haley exclaim, 'Oh, here it is!' The necklace had been lying at the side of her bed. At that point I broke out into fluent French.

The only genuine household injury Sooty sustained was when my son shut the freezer door with Sooty's tail half in it. The said tail had a kink in the middle for a while, but eventually managed to rectify itself.

Sooty's normal, but not fixed, routine was to stay in during the evening. He had two favourite spots on which he rested in the living room. One was on a bean bag beside the window, which constantly had to be plumped up and hollowed at the top to avoid him sliding off. The rustling that it made when he changed position is still in my ears. It was strangely comforting. The other spot he liked was on the two-seater settee which was at right angles to the three-seater that I lay on. I would regularly look across at him as he lay cosily curled up beside the arm. He often seemed to sense that, and, without raising his head, he would look back at me. There was something in those exchanges that defies definition.

He habitually went out at our bedtime, and could be out all night (though mostly in the summer), but it was not unusual for him to come knocking on my bedroom window in the early hours of the morning. Was I allowed to ignore him? No. The drubbing on the pane with his paws just carried on at regular intervals until his will was met. Then I would have to get out of a nice, warm bed, go to the kitchen door and call and whistle for him. Would he come? Often, no. I would be forced to do a barefoot walk round the back of the house in the pitch black until he eventually decided to respond. And when he did come in, it was frequently just for a top-up feed, and I would have to stand waiting for him to satisfy his appetite before acting as commissionaire again. I cursed him roundly for it. Another habit he had was to insist on being admitted through the front door only to gallop directly to the back door to be let out again. Figure that one out. I could have throttled him at times, but I would gladly tolerate the broken sleep and other inconveniences for the rest of my life just to have him with us still.

As with Magic, the end came suddenly and unexpectedly. One moment Sooty seemed fine, as fit as a fiddle, then the next he was off his food and reluctant to come into the house. This was in early September 2016. In the warmer months, I always imagined that he ate less anyway, but I had never known him to eat little or nothing at all. Neither had he stayed away from the house for more than a few hours at a time, even in the summer, in all the years with us; but, for a couple of days, he only came back once, briefly. On the third day, he didn't come back at all, so in the morning I went out and started calling for him. He didn't come. I walked to the bottom of the back garden and peered through the hedge. I could see him lying in the adjoining garden and I knew then that something was wrong. He would not have heard me call and not responded. We no longer had a cat carrier, so I had to improvise with a lidded plastic storage container, making the necessary air vents. Having telephoned the veterinary clinic to make an urgent appointment, I then drove round to the house where he was. It had electric gates which were closed. I pressed the buzzer, but got no response. Luckily, the woman who lived there came out of a detached outbuilding and spotted me standing at the gates with the box under my arm. The driveway was so long that it seemed to take an age for her to reach me.

'I think our cat is ill and lying in your garden,' I explained.

She let me in and, when I got to Sooty, he tried to escape, but didn't have the strength. I got him into the container and drove straight to the clinic.

It wasn't Linda who saw to Sooty, but a pleasant young woman called Hatty. I was expecting the worst because Sooty was panting a lot, but Hatty thought there was an outside chance that he had an infection and that all was not necessarily lost. Having taken blood tests and an X-ray, she administered an injection and told me to bring him straight back in the morning if he got worse.

It was a long night. When I got him home, Sooty made his way into the front bedroom and collapsed on the floor. He stayed there all evening but, when I got up to check on him during the night, he had moved to the mat at the front door, a familiar resting place for him in the past. In the very early hours of the morning he was lying just inside the living room, panting heavily and obviously struggling for breath. I got a bowl of water, wet my finger, and rubbed it round his gums. I stroked him and talked to him, all the while feeling quite helpless. Over the course of the morning, though he was struggling to walk, he made his way from one room to the next in a complete circuit, ending up in my bedroom. The injection hadn't helped him and I knew that this was the end. It appeared to me that he had been saying goodbye to all his familiar spots in turn, and that overwhelmed me with emotion.

As soon as the clinic opened, I took Sooty in immediately. The X-ray had shown an extensive blockage in his chest and, effectively, all hope was indeed gone. Hatty said that she would put him on a drip in the meantime until we got organised to come and say our goodbyes. I wanted to wait until my son was home from school, but it was intimated to me that Sooty might not, or ought not to made to last that long. So, Haley and I went back to see him one final time. I gently stroked his head and softly spoke into his ear, saying, with my voice cracking with emotion, 'You'll never know how much I love you.' He may not have understood the words, but I am convinced he sensed the meaning of them, for he gave a little short, sharp miaow in response. In the meantime, Linda had heard what was happening and came to offer comfort, which was greatly appreciated. Once again, I could not face the final moments, so I left the room.

My son was shocked at the news and upset that he couldn't be there. He got me to ring the clinic to ask if they would clip some of Sooty's fur, a little of the black and white, for him to keep as a memento. Hatty was happy to oblige and we went down that evening to collect it. We also arranged to have his ashes returned to us.

Now I must emphasise that I am not an emotional man as a rule. Some would even be surprised to learn that

I have any emotions at all. I had only cried once before in my adult life, when Magic died, but Sooty's death brought me to tears again. Every time I thought of his last night in the house, and the final farewell, I just broke down, so I had to force myself not to think of it. That was my way of coping. It took years before I could bring myself to look at photographs of Magic and Cutie. It helped too that I was busy at the time organising the clearance and sale of my father's house. That was a forced distraction. However, in writing this account I am only too aware that not enough time has yet elapsed for me to remember Sooty with equanimity.

I should also say that neither am I a man given to fantasy or wishful thinking. I would regard myself as a sceptic when it comes to human delusion and sentimentality. My childhood saw to that. But nothing will shake me from the conviction that Sooty was trying to convey his feelings to me at the end. Love is not something that can be *proved*. It can only be *sensed*. And I sensed it.

What age Sooty was when he died is unknown. My guess is that he may only have been about ten. He was certainly a young cat when he first turned up because he did later develop an audible miaow and his head eventually assumed a more sensible proportion to the rest of his body. I think my heart had always gone out to him because one way or another he had been abandoned, but I am glad he chose to stay with us and that we had the opportunity to care for him for the rest of his life.

Chapter 12

An Interlude

In the months following Sooty's death I was largely pre-occupied with sorting out my late father's affairs. He had left his house to the grandchildren but I, as his executor, was handed the privilege of clearing it and dealing with its sale. I thought I was at least going to get a lawnmower out of it, but it turned out that his was broken too. If nothing else, it all helped divert my attention and prevented me from dwelling on the loss of Sooty. But, of course, there are always little reminders at home in the quiet times, especially in the early days. I stopped sitting at the back of the house for weeks, otherwise I would visualise him trotting across the grass towards me; he had had the habit of joining me on the patio steps. There were his favourite sleeping spots in the garden too, which pained me to look at. Inside, I continued to glance at the kitchen door in case he wanted in. Fur on the carpet, scratches on the wallpaper, paw marks on the windows—these were all triggers of sadness, but, irrationally, I didn't want them removed. When I came home one day to discover that Haley had taken away his feeding dishes from the kitchen floor, I sought them out and put them back. I wasn't ready to let go yet. In the evenings, I missed watching him lie contentedly on the settee and hearing him resettle on his bean bag.

Gradually, however, I started to get used to not having

him about. By December, 2016, my father's possessions had been sorted, the house cleared and the sale all but completed. My son and I began to have conversations about the possibility of finding another cat, but I had reservations. Much as I had loved all our cats, Magic, Cutie and Sooty were often in and out all through the night. I had been the one hopping out of bed to see to them and I wasn't getting any younger. Why didn't we get a cat flap? To avoid carnage inside the house. In the summer, we had been in the habit of leaving windows open, not just for the air, but to let Magic and Cutie come and go as they pleased. But dolls' heads apart, they (normally Cutie) would proudly bring mice and birds to show us. Try getting a magpie out of a bedroom when it is going berserk. So, admittance became regulated. Henceforth, Cutie would bring her catches to the doors. Although it was difficult to see through the patterned glass, I always knew when she had a mouse because she emitted a low, tell-tale growl.

Having cats also restricted my freedom. Apart from the countless hours lost because I felt too guilty to move a settled cat from my legs or lap, the reluctance to change from an uncomfortable position in bed for fear of disturbing my sleeping companion, it made going away difficult too. We have only ever had two vacations, in 2004 and 2005, for about ten days on each occasion. In a telephone conversation with an old friend from my days in the RAF in the early 1980s, we discussed the possibility of our two families going on holiday together in France. Being a Francophile, the idea appealed to me, but I really couldn't afford it. Martin said, 'If you wait until you have the money then you'll probably never go.' He was right. So, I threw caution to the wind and took the holiday on credit. However, there was Cutie to consider. I had been with her every day of her life thus far and I worried about leaving her. I needed to know that she would be well looked after. Thankfully, I had a good friend, Colette, another bookseller, who knew Cutie and was genuinely delighted at being asked to look after her. She took Cutie to her house, about six miles away, for the duration. The holiday was thoroughly enjoyable, so we decided to do it all again in the next summer, and Colette looked after Cutie once again. Colette sadly passed away recently, and I am sorry that she did not live to read these words. On both occasions that I brought Cutie home, she nervously explored the house, almost as though she was seeing it for the first time.

There was the financial aspect to be considered too. Over the latter years, it had become harder and harder to scratch a living from bookselling. The collectors in my field of speciality had virtually all died and no young ones emerged to replace them. Book collecting generally was in sharp decline and competition online had increased to the point where it was hard to buy in any stock without the risk of having to sell at a loss. Prices for most of the relatively common books had dropped to virtually nothing and many of the rarer books were being made digitally available for free. In general terms, only collectors would be prepared pay good money for an original hard copy book when the text was easily accessible online, and collectors are now very thin on the ground. It came to the point where I was earning so little from bookselling, or perhaps even operating at a loss, that I decided that it wasn't worth the effort anymore, and began disposing of the stock to other dealers for whatever I could get. I had long since ceased to be fit enough to do a milk round, although that trade had virtually vanished anyway, so I had to think of another way to generate an income. In the end, I began to focus on publishing, mostly historical reprints, and started to design and typeset for other authors. I was effectively starting from scratch and the building process was painfully slow. Haley, meanwhile, went back into the job market after an absence of some years, and took work as a care assistant, earning what I regard as a relative pittance for the hours and tasks involved. But beggars can't be choosers, and we keep rolling on regardless.

The lack of sufficient income has meant that the house is steadily falling into a state of disrepair. The water from a leak in the roof is collected in a biscuit tin strategically placed in the attic; a couple of electric sockets have ceased to work; windows don't close properly and are taped round the edges to (unsuccessfully) prevent drafts; fixtures and fittings badly need replaced; the beautiful back garden is now a veritable wilderness of grass and weeds.

I write all this not to elicit sympathy, because I am inexplicably confident that, given time, the situation can be turned around. Like the impecunious Mr Micawber, from Dickens's novel *David Copperfield*, I have faith that 'something will turn up'. It generally does. No, I am merely trying to establish reasons for my reticence to take on another cat. The cost of feeding one would be negligible, but I had to consider the possibility that the cat might get injured or become ill. The expense of having it treated would not be met easily.

To continue the tale of woe, I wish I could say that at least I still have my health, but I can't. In 2010, at the age of fifty, I suffered a heart attack. I was in the bathroom having a wash and had just sprayed deodorant under my arms when I felt pain in my chest and my throat started to burn. Assuming this was the result of ingesting the deodorant, I went to the kitchen and began to drink copious amounts of water; but no relief came. I ended up crouched on the floor on my hands and knees, in great agony. Haley rang the doctor on call. When she described the burning sensation in my throat, he said, 'Oh, it's got to that stage. Ring for an ambulance.' Mercifully, the cardiac crew were with me in next to no time, administered drugs, took readings, and transported me to the Ulster Hospital in Dundonald. A few days later, I was transferred to Belfast City Hospital to have an angiogram. I was informed beforehand that one in every thousand of this operation goes wrong. Well, the 999 people before me should count themselves lucky. I never did find out exactly what the problem was, but things did go awry, a second surgeon was called in, and the whole affair seemed to drag on for an eternity. It wasn't painful as such, but I experienced an overwhelming discomfort in my chest, so much so that after a while I was close to just wanting to die and be done with it. I never saw her face or heard her name, but the nurse who was administering the sedatives kept hold of my hand the whole time. She will never know how much that meant to me. I had five stents put in to keep my arteries open. The next meal I had was the one I relished most in my life but, strangely, I can't recall what it was.

I had three more heart attacks after that, almost in successive years, and a couple more hospital admissions that turned out just to be stress related. Not that I wish to repeat the experience, but my sojourns in hospital were not entirely unenjoyable. In fact, I hadn't laughed so much since I was in the barrack block in the Royal Air Force nearly 30 years before. On each stay, I was fortunate enough to share a bay with some old Belfast characters, a seemingly disappearing breed, who were full of wit and banter. I was explaining to a newcomer that 'There are two heart wards—Ward 16 and Ward 20—but I don't know what the difference is.' Then I heard a little voice pipe up from the corner, 'Four.' It was the septuagenarian Cecil, an ex-shipyard worker and greyhound breeder. I had walked straight into that.

I feel very grateful to all those good people who aided my recovery—too numerous to name individually. The National Health Service is one institution of which the British people ought to be very proud. Without it I would not be alive today. Long may it continue. For what sort of society would we have if we did not care for our sick and elderly, irrespective of circumstances?

A consequence of my heart condition was I could no longer assume that I would even live to see the next day. Naturally, I hope to have a good few years left yet, but it is not something that can be taken for granted. All it might take is for me to be in the wrong place at the wrong time, or the ambulance to be delayed, and I would be history. That it is not morbidity, but a realistic possibility which must be faced. It is not something that bothers me unduly. We've all got to go sometime, as the old cliché goes. On one of my hospital stays, I had the bed opposite a man who read the Bible practically all through the day and whose life revolved around his church. When I met him at cardiac rehabilitation some months later I was struck by how he lived in dread fear of every pain and twinge. I remember thinking that if I was bound for the same destination I'd feel a lot less apprehensive at the prospect.

After my death-defying adventures, decisions that had long-term implications had to be thought through very carefully, and that included adopting another cat. My son would leave home at some point, and there was no guarantee that Haley would be in a position to look after the cat if I was gone. The house might have to be sold for a start.

All these matters had to be taken into consideration. However, there was another, more positive angle to take. I hadn't had an 'episode' in over 18 months, not even a twinge, in fact. Up until Sooty died, which threw me out of kilter, I was setting off at 6 am every morning for a two-mile walk along Ballyholme beach, and had shed excess weight. I was much fitter than I'd been for many years. Another old chum from my RAF days, Rick, now a doctor in California, had told me of a man he knew who had heart attacks in his fifties and was still very physically active now in his nineties. My father had heart attacks and he lived until he was eighty. Having expressed my concerns about taking on another cat to my mother, now in her eighties too, she said, 'You can't think like that'. She encouraged me to adopt a more positive outlook and so, I did. None of our cats had been insured, but a little insurance wouldn't break the bank and it would cover against any unexpected bills. As for the personal inconveniences, from my long experience they were far outweighed by the pleasures that a cat could bring to a home.

So, I decided to gamble on the positive side. On balance, I was prepared to serve yet another master, although I would try to train the next one into staying in at nights.

Chapter 13

Assisi Animal Sanctuary

The Assisi Animal Sanctuary at Conlig was only several miles away, so around lunchtime on 3 January 2017, my son Thomas and I took a trip over to look at the cats. At the reception, I filled in a form with my personal details and answered a questionnaire, then we made our way up to the cattery. At right angles to the main building was an extension with wire grill sides that allowed the cats to get fresh air. Inside there was furniture and different types of climbing frames to keep the guests occupied and happy. We stood watching for a while and our attention was particularly drawn to a couple of young and lively black and white cats. Running horizontally along the centre of the mesh was a ledge on to which a small tabby jumped right in front of us and began to miaow loudly as if to say, 'What about me?' It was a cute little thing, no doubt about it.

As it was lunchtime, the member of staff looking after the main cattery was on a break, but there was someone in attendance in a smaller adjoining section. She opened the door and asked us to disinfect our shoes in a foot bath before entering. Once inside, we had a good look at the cats in each cubicle.

'What sort of cat are you looking for?' the girl asked.

'I'm not quite sure,' I replied, 'but I would like it to be particularly good-natured.'

Following a little further conversation, she said, 'From what you have told me, this one might be suitable,' and she proceeded to open the door of one of the cubicles that housed a black cat.

'This is what I get every morning,' she said, as it stretched forward to nuzzle her.

She told me he was called King Noel, and that he had been found wandering around Holburn Avenue in central Bangor. I presumed that he was given that name because he was brought in over Christmas.

Then I rather stupidly said, 'He seems affectionate, but I wasn't really looking for a black cat.' Of all people, I should have known better. Yes, I found some cats more pleasing to the eye than others, but one grows to love a cat because of its personality, not its colour. There may have been some psychology involved too. Perhaps I was resistant to the choice, even if it was a right one, because it was suggested to me. The human mind is an unfathomable mystery at times. Many years ago, I read a biography of Billy Butlin, the founder of the Butlin's holiday camps, and can remember nothing in it now except one anecdote concerning his early career. The details are hazy, but he had set up a hoopla stall outside a venue at a major event and was offering live puppies as prizes. Long queues of people formed, desperate to win one of the dogs, and he was lifting a fortune. Then the event organiser raised objections to the stall and, not knowing what else he could do with them, Butlin was forced to give the puppies away for free, but, try as he might, he couldn't get any takers. He learned something from that.

We went back outside and wandered around for a

while. There were two square outbuildings, isolated from the main cattery, that also housed cats. In one of these sat an older woman who I assumed was a volunteer visitor. When she came out, she asked,

'Is nobody seeing to you?'

I explained that we had been attended to, but we were waiting to go into the main cattery.

'I'll go and get Caroline,' she said.

'No, no,' I replied. 'Don't disturb her if she is having lunch. We can wait.'

'But it's cold out.'

'It's not that bad, and we're well wrapped up.'

She set off for the reception area anyway.

Not long afterwards, Caroline came along and let us in to see the other cats. The ones immediately through the door were in cubicles, but in the adjoining room others were roaming about freely. The little tabby cat that had been miaowing to us from the annex approached me, resting her front paws on my knee as I squatted down.

'That's Tegan,' said Caroline.

'Oh, yes. We met her outside. I'd seen her on your website too,' I said. 'She's very friendly. How come she ended up here?'

Caroline explained that Tegan and her sister Trixie had originally been Assisi kittens. A woman had given them both a home for five years, but then recently had children who developed allergies to them, so she had to bring the cats back.

'She was distraught when she left them off,' continued Caroline.

'I can understand that,' I said. 'I've been in a similar position myself.'

Meanwhile Thomas was stroking some of the other cats, including Trixie, who was curled up comfortably in a basket. She was a hotchpotch of white, tabby and tortoiseshell. The black and white cats were hovering about too, but they were too preoccupied with their own affairs to pay us much attention.

'We'll go for a walk to think things over,' I said to Caroline after a while. 'There are so many lovely cats to choose from.'

Thomas and I wandered out of the sanctuary and down the road towards the car. He had lost his voice at the time, so his side of the discussion was croaked. We liked the idea of having another black and white cat if only to keep the tradition going, but Tegan was a cute little thing and evidently very affectionate. However, Caroline had said that Tegan and Trixie were to be rehomed together, so that would mean double the expense and possibly double trouble. We returned to the cattery still undecided.

Back inside, I sat down on the floor and called and beckoned Tegan unto my lap. She made a few tentative approaches before finally hopping on. She twisted and turned and purred and nestled.

'It looks like she's picked you,' said Caroline.

'It seems that way,' I replied, 'but I can't believe how small she is for five.'

Compared with Sooty, she appeared almost like a kitten in size.

Thomas was back with Trixie and I got up and went over.

She was still lying curled up in her basket, but did eventually sit up and let out a contented miaow. She seemed like a placid little cat.

'Decision made?' I asked, turning to Thomas.

He nodded.

'It looks like it's going to be Tegan and Trixie then,' I said to Caroline.

Before we left the sanctuary, I was told that a home visitor would call out to see us, probably within a couple of days. That was on the Tuesday. I waited impatiently until Thursday afternoon before giving Assisi a ring to find out if an appointment was imminent and I got talking to a girl called Suzie. Someone had been assigned to us, I was informed, and would be in touch shortly. I had another reason for calling though. Since our visit to the cattery I had not been able to get King Noel out of my mind. I had dismissed him out of hand, without due consideration. When I thought about him later, and how he was a stray like Sooty, I began to feel really bad. I asked about him on the phone.

'Why?' asked Suzie. 'Are you thinking of taking him instead of Tegan and Trixie?'

'No, no,' I reassured her, 'but he's such a good-natured boy that I hate to think of him not having a good home.

What was really in my head was that I wished I had parallel lives so that I could have Tegan and Trixie in one and King Noel in the other. Taking on a third cat was not something that I wanted to do, but if push came to shove then I would. Still, I thought, it would be better that King Noel quickly found another home, if only to

Our first meeting with Tegan at Assisi Animal Sanctuary

Trixie in her bed at Assisi

assuage my guilt and get me off the hook. I racked my brains to think how I might help in that respect, but the only thing I could think of was to post about him online. In the end, it wasn't necessary.

In the late afternoon, I got a call from a woman called Tracy, our designated home visitor from Assisi.

'When suits you?' she asked, after the preliminary exchanges were made.

'Whenever suits you.'

'What about this evening?'

'Not a problem. What time?'

'About 6.30?'

'Yep, fine.'

We had an hour or two to try to make the house look respectable—an exercise in optimism, if ever there was one. At least she was coming when it was dark, and we had low wattage bulbs fitted.

Tracy arrived bang on time and I showed her into the living room where Thomas and Haley were already sitting. She posed the requisite questions and got us to sign an agreement. Then she asked to see the back garden.

'Close your eyes on the way through to the kitchen,' I said. 'The house is a bit of a shambles.'

'We're not worried about that,' she replied, reassuringly.

Outside it was too dark for her to see that the felt had been stripped from the roof of the shed and that the door had fallen off. It was propped up by a ladder. You could just about discern the outline of the surrounding hedge.

'Is the garden completely enclosed?' she asked.

'Yes, but there are plenty ways to escape, if they wanted

to,' I replied honestly, thinking it might be a black mark against us.

Tracy had to get to another appointment, so I saw her to her car after that.

'Look,' I said, 'whatever Assisi decides is fine with me. I will understand.'

The next day I received a call from Suzie.

'I believe Tracy was with you last night. Would you like to collect Tegan and Trixie tomorrow at 2.30?'

'Yes, not a problem.'

I was over the moon that we'd passed muster, but disappointed not to bring the cats home that same day.

It must be said that I'd initially had reservations about going through all the formalities of homing a cat from the sanctuary, especially concerning the home visit. That was before my brain got into gear and I thought things through properly. Assisi invests time and money in caring for their animals, which are all given whatever treatment is required to make and keep them healthy. By ethos, it has a sense of responsibility towards them too. It is therefore only reasonable that good care is taken as to whom and where they go. The woman who had to bring Tegan and Trixie back to the sanctuary did so, I'm sure, because she knew this to be the case. How would she feel if just anyone was allowed to take her girls away without checks? How would I feel if I were in that position? No, at the end of the day, I am very glad that I went to Assisi. The sanctuary is spotlessly clean and so are the cats. They couldn't be better looked after.

I arrived half an hour early on the Saturday. Suzie was on the desk and she told me that King Noel had since been booked, which was terrific news. I was in the process of making a voluntary payment for the cats when Caroline arrived at the reception and took the two carriers we had bought. By the time I caught up with her at the cattery she and a couple of assistants, in the face of some resistance, were putting Tegan and Trixie into them. That mission finally accomplished, Caroline carried Trixie and I took Tegan to the car.

Tegan lay quietly during the short journey. Trixie was vocal all the way, but a long way short of being in Cutie's league.

When I got home, I took them into the living room, where Thomas, Haley and I together released them into their new domain.

Chapter 14

Tegan and Trixie

Trixie was the surprise package. She immediately and systematically set about exploring the rooms, crawling into every nook, sniffing at every cranny, and sizing up potential jumps. The day was punctuated by the sound of a variety of items getting knocked off tables and shelves around the house. If curiosity was ever going to kill a cat, I thought, it would be her. She was in the bath, down the toilet, and even contemplated a trip up the chimney. She wandered about happily with her tail in the air, as if to say, 'Party time!'. She truly seemed to be having a ball. Her tabby tail, by the way, with its wonderful curl at the end, could easily be mistaken for a transplant from another cat—it is so different from her body. As a neighbour put it, 'It looks like it's been stuck on.' Anyway, getting back to the point, whatever else Trixie might be, shy and placid she is not.

Tegan, on the other hand, was less inquisitive and much more cautious. Attention was what she was after. I made myself available as her bed for as much as of the day as possible, but, if I left her, she hunted me down like a heat-seeking missile. If I gave her a momentary opportunity, she would clamber onto me, so I was forced to tie my shoe laces standing up whenever I needed to go out. Whereas Trixie was practically oblivious to our movements, Tegan would dart for cover if anyone came near. Trixie willingly raised her head to meet the hand that went to pet her, but Tegan ducked away.

Until they were properly settled we couldn't risk letting them outside for exercise, so Thomas and I used a toy mouse on a piece of string to tire them out before bedtime or, more accurately, to tire Trixie out. She didn't need much encouragement to play, and was lightning quick. I had never seen such a fast and agile cat. She jumped and chased until she got caught that mouse and then gave it 'what for' when she did.

'She'll make a good mouser,' I remarked to Thomas. And I wasn't wrong.

That was Trixie. Tegan, however, couldn't have cared less. For the most part, she followed the dangled mouse with her eyes, but otherwise didn't move a muscle.

The differences in personality were already very apparent. In fact, if I hadn't been told, I would never have guessed that they were from the same litter. They are so different physically too. Apart from her white muzzle, underbelly and paws, Tegan is entirely tabby, and a muscular girl too, with a thin, tapering little tail. Trixie is an irregular patchwork quilt of tortoiseshell and tabby on top, with a comparatively long, bushy tail. Her fur is so soft, and there is so little substance at the core, that I think of her as the candy floss cat. Haley remarked that Tegan has beautiful eyes. She does. Trixie has comparatively small, green eyes, with little diamond slit pupils. Tegan's pupils are habitually dilated like big, dark, round pools.

That first night the two slept on the living room settee,

good as gold, until the morning. For the following few nights there was a game of musical beds, involving the living room, Haley's room and mine. The established routine currently is that Trixie sleeps in the middle of my bed, so that I am obliged to lie at an angle or with my legs spread open, and Tegan snoozes on the chair beside me.

On the tenth morning I woke up alone and wandered into the living room to see Trixie with a mouse in her mouth. Tegan was in close attendance.

'I knew it! Good girl!' I said.

Haley retrieved the catch and released it in the garden. If it has any sense, that mouse won't come back.

After a couple of days, Trixie didn't know what to be at. She seemed to be going stir crazy. The sooner I get her used to going outside, the better, I thought. So, with some misgivings, I let her out into the back garden to do a little exploration. My theory was that, not knowing the territory she'd be cautious and not go too far. I was right. I gave her about 15 minutes then brought her in again. The next day, Tuesday, I repeated the experiment with the same success. On Wednesday, I thought I'd let her out the front door to better familiarise her with the geography of the house. It all went well until I tried to lift her in again. She bolted. I then found myself at 57 years of age, with a dodgy heart, leaping over garden walls like an Olympic hurdler in a vain attempt to catch her. At one point, I thought I had her cornered against a neighbour's wall, but she shot off in the opposite direction like greased lightning and I completely lost sight of her. I walked back in a state of panic, but, looking round the side of the house, I spotted her again.

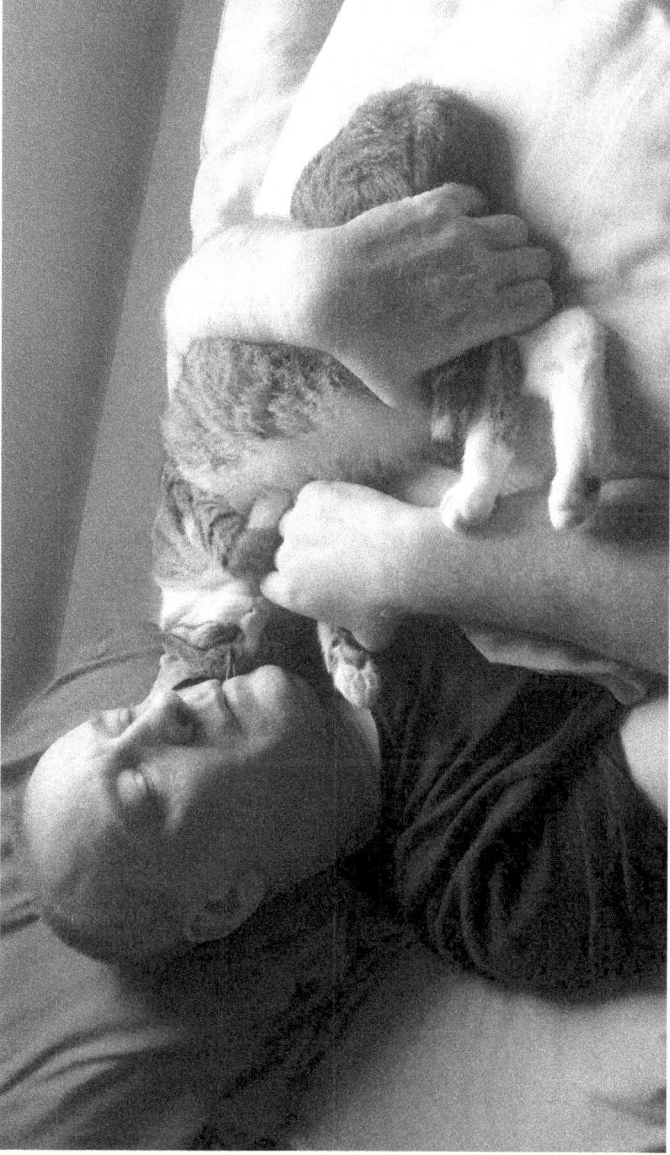

Tegan resting with the author. Tegan is the one on the right.

Trixie with her 'stuck on' tail carrying on a Sooty tradition

I called. She came. I reincarcerated her in the house.

Now, the fact that she had responded to my call was a jolly good sign, but I wasn't in a hurry to repeat the experience. I kept her in on Thursday. Trixie, however, had the scent of freedom in her nostrils. At about 9.30 that night I realised that I hadn't seen her for a while so, after a quick look around, I went to Haley.

'Where's Trixie?' I asked.

'I haven't seen her.'

A thorough search was then conducted. No sign. I began to suspect the worst.

'Have you been outside tonight?'

'I put some bottles in the bin,' Haley confirmed.

'When was that?'

'About half an hour ago.'

'Oh, hell!' I said. 'I'll bet she's slipped out.'

For over an hour we took turns to stand outside in the dark and freezing cold to call for her. But Trixie didn't come. 'Oh, great!' I thought. 'How will I explain this to Assisi?'

At a quarter to eleven I was in the process of putting a duvet and some pillows on the kitchen floor to prepare for a long vigil when, to my delight and great relief, Trixie's little face appeared at the door.

That escape was a blessing in disguise. It established that Trixie already saw this as her home and could find her way back.

There was, however, one thing that puzzled me. Almost as soon as she was through the door, Trixie made use of the litter tray. She had been away for nearly two hours, so why hadn't she 'gone' outside? I began to wonder if Tegan and Trixie had been house cats previously or, at least, lived in an urban area where toilet provisions were few. Sooty never had need of a litter tray. So, the next morning, we dug up part of what used to be a flower bed and scattered litter on it. That afternoon we watched with satisfaction through the kitchen window as Trixie availed herself of the new facility. After a month, the indoor tray is still being used, but less and less frequently.

Tegan was offered her freedom over the weekend, but refused to take it. She sniffed at the open door for a while then turned and walked away. It wasn't until the following Monday that she finally took the plunge, and she didn't look back after that. Well, technically, I suppose, she did look back, otherwise we wouldn't have seen her again. But you know what I mean. Trixie generally comes when she is called now, but Tegan only returns when it suits her.

When it comes to visitors to the house, Trixie is her usual oblivious self. She just carries on regardless. It is too early to tell for sure but, so far, Tegan has shied away from the women and made a beeline for the men. She even insisted on sitting on the lap of my old friend Gordon, despite my every effort to keep her off. He likes to say that he is 'wary' of cats. I prefer to say *scared stiff*.

In the weeks that she has been with us, Trixie has been a constant source of entertainment. There have been many 'Come and see this!' moments. We watched in amazement as she came clambering through the bathroom window and slid down the inside. No mean feat. She has come flying out from under a table causing an explosion of pot

Top Cat

Trixie window-gazing

pourri as she brought the tablecloth with her. A 50-year-old lamp was the only casualty. Thomas had been rather injudicious in his use of the toy mouse. In the garden, she is ever on the alert, with her head jolting from side to side and her ears constantly twitching. No passing insect is safe from her leap. So like Magic and so unlike Sooty—a bomb could have exploded beside him and he'd have paid no heed. Inside, Trixie crouches down behind doors with her backside wiggling, ready to pounce on an unsuspecting Tegan as she wanders past. Tegan is not always amused. When it comes to food, there are parallels with Magic too. Feed Trixie first and she will leave off eating to investigate what Tegan is given immediately after; and my meals are attended and closely scrutinised too. Then there are her funny half hours when she randomly bolts around the house, chasing and pouncing on imaginary mice.

Yes, Trixie has been a surprise package and an absolute delight. She shows every sign of being happy with her lot.

Tegan is an entirely different personality. She is much more sedate and less confident, although she is gradually coming out of her shell. She is becoming more relaxed and plays a bit now, even having the occasional funny half hour herself, but, essentially, she is just a little love machine. Trixie will turn two or three times before flopping down on me and instantaneously fall asleep. Tegan will gently knead away before she settles—in great contrast to Sooty's kneading, which was akin to receiving treatment from a sadistic acupuncturist and required epic endurance. In the mornings, when I sit down in front of the computer to begin my day's work, that is Tegan's cue to hop on my lap to receive some tender, loving care. She is on my knee now as I type these words. If I stop stroking her she looks up at me to ask why.

The weather has been cold, blustery and wet during their first month here, but, come the summer, the girls will think they are in paradise. I look forward to their further adventures and, if they come home with swollen faces, I will know with what I am dealing. It will take a while for our lives to harmonize perfectly, as it did with the other cats, but it will happen gradually and imperceptibly, I'm sure.

I could write so much more about Tegan and Trixie and their little ways, but you, the reader, might become afflicted with OPCS (Other People's Cats Syndrome—see the Preface). So, here I will bring my humble account to a close.

Chapter 15

Of Cats and Men

It has always seemed to me that whereas dogs appeal to both men and women equally, cats are more commonly associated with women. Nevertheless, there are numerous examples in literature and history of men who were particularly devoted to their cats. Not so long ago I disposed of most of the many thousands of books that I had, but I still hold onto quite a wide selection. On browsing through the 1903 annual of *The Quiver* magazine, looking for something else entirely, I stumbled across an interesting article on cats, 'God's Beautiful Creatures', by Rev. Hugh Macmillan. In it were references to famous and not so famous men who were known to be cat-lovers. Apart from the fact that the piece was so beautifully crafted, there was so much else of relevance in it to what I had written and was about to write about cats that I make no apology for quoting extensively from it here. On the variation in cat personalities, Rev. Macmillan had this to say:

> 'There are not nearly so many breeds of cats as of dogs; and most cats have a wonderful resemblance to one another, from the tabby to the Persian. Owing to this general likeness, we are apt to imagine that their character is also very much the same. But while they all have the typical cat-nature in large measure, each animal, if closely observed, has a certain degree of individual peculiarity. He who attentively

studies their little ways finds that they have many interesting personal traits, which identify them more even than
outward appearance. We once had a very graceful grey cat,
which, without any teaching, instinctively fetched and carried things. It loved to run for a quill thrown at a distance,
and bring it back in its mouth, and lay it at one's feet; and
it would repeat this time after time with unerring certainty.
Its favourite amusement was to abstract the pens from my
desk, to sit beside me while I was writing, and watch with
a wise look every stroke I made, and even with its soft,
outstretched paw pat my pen as it scribbled on the paper:
an attention somewhat distracting! How did this pussy
acquire so strange a habit? Was it a sporadic inheritance
from the far past ages, when its ancestors in Egypt were
employed to hunt, as the cheetah is in India at the present
day, before the animal was domesticated? We had another
cat, of Spanish descent, a splendid large sleek creature,
with black stripes upon its dark grey body, which could
do a great many tricks, give a paw, turn head over heels,
and die for its country. Alas! it soon suffered the fate of too
many domestic pets; and we noticed how a primitive habit
came out in this highly educated cat. A day or two before
it died it disappeared, and could not be found. At last we
discovered it in the bath, where it had hidden itself. This
seems to be not an uncommon instinct of cats, and is a
certain precursor of death. Social animals in a wild state
leave the company of their fellows at the approach of death,
and seek some solitary spot, in order to escape being torn
to pieces, as the ill or wounded creature is apt to be by its
fellows, and die in peace.

Cats have shown the extremes of cruelty and devotion
to their offspring. We read of a London cat that crawled
four times under the stage of a burning theatre to rescue

her kittens, and perished with the fifth in her endeavour to bring it to a place of safety. And, on the other hand, we read of a cat drowning its kittens in a water-butt to save herself the trouble of bringing them up. Theophilus Gautier, who was a great lover of cats, had one particular pet, called Éponine, which sat with him at table at dinner. He says of her that she went regularly through all the courses of the meal, from soup to dessert, awaiting her turn to be helped, and behaving all the time with a dignified propriety.'

Thinking of Sooty's behaviour in his last days, I was particularly struck and touched by the author's description of how one of his cats had gone off to die alone. I had heard of this before, thinking that it might only be an urban myth, but there it was in black and white, and with a plausible explanation.

Rev. Macmillan proceeded later in the article to give the following examples of famous men from history who were particularly devoted to cats:

'The cat has been honourably mentioned in connection with men who have made history. Cardinal Wolsey, while Lord High Chancellor of England, loved to work with a magnificent cat that sat in a cushioned armchair by his side, and seemed to reflect in its grand air his pomp and pride. Richelieu also delighted in caressing his favourite cat; and Micatto, a gift to Chateaubriand from the Pope, often soothed his troubled spirits by its antics. Sainte-Beuve, Baudelaire, and Theophilus Gautier had their literary labours lightened by the presence of a little furry friend, who sat on their desks, roamed at will among their manuscripts, and flopped its ringed tail across their "copy."

Montaigne said regarding his cat, "When I play with her, how do I know that she does not make a jest of me? We entertain each other with mutual tricks." Lord Chesterfield found something suitable to his cynical temperament in the association of an animal which maintained its own aloofness, and had no need of human company, while it suffered his blandishments and claimed his intimacy and confidence with a proud disdain. Sir Walter Scott had a much valued cat called Master Hinse at Abbotsford; and on one occasion, when feeling the loneliness of a London inn, he wrote home: "There are no dogs in the hotel where I lodge, but a tolerably conversable cat, who eats a mess of cream with me in the morning." And President Lincoln found frequent relief from the overwhelming cares of state, during the terrible times of the Civil War in America, in the gracious attentions of his pretty little cat, to which he often alluded in his conversations with his friends.'

And of men of literature and art who made affectionate studies of the cat, he observed:

'Poets have sung almost from time immemorial the praises of the cat, from the pretty gambollings of the innocent kitten—surely one of the most graceful and beautiful objects in creation—to the staid dignity and composure of the most experienced puss, which looks at a string or a ball at its feet, wondering if it had ever seen it before. Wordsworth in his poem on "The Kitten and Falling Leaves" refers with touching simplicity to its want of self-consciousness in its play, "overwealthy in the treasure of its own exceeding pleasure." Heine gives us a graphic picture of the purring cat increasing the cosiness of his fireside, "wrapping his mind in a realm of dreams." And Shelley notices how essential to the feeling of home-enjoyment is the drowsy cat coiled on the hearth-stone, in a letter to Peacock, in which he depicts the worship of the Penates as consisting of "the purring of kittens, the singing of kettles, the long talks over the past and dead, the laugh of children, the warm wind of summer filling the quiet house, and the pelting storm of winter struggling in vain for entrance." Some of the most graceful of the poetic tributes evoked by this "cat-cult" are contained in a small but charming anthology gathered by Mrs. Graham R. Thomson, entitled "Concerning Cats," wherein we find a few delightful verses by herself conjoined with dainty selections from the French of Baudelaire, Cowper's graphic fireside sketch of "The Retired Cat," and Calverly's "Sad Memories," recording the sincere grief often caused to many a home and heart by the departure of creatures whose presence while living added so much to the happiness of domestic life.

We might expect that an animal so much petted, whose every feature and movement are full of vivacity and grace, would be a favourite subject of the artist's pencil. Many have attained high eminence in this department of art—such as Burbank, the celebrated English painter of cats; Cornelius Wisseler, the Dutch limner; Delacroix, the French artist, whose sketchbook was full of studies of cats; and Hokusu, the Japanese genius. Madame Henriette Ronner has paint-ed to the very life the irresistible ways of the fascinating animals; and Mr. M. H. Spielmann in an exquisite volume has described in glowing terms, illustrated by numerous lovely examples from her facile pencil, their many claims to our admiration and love. Arthur Thomson exhibited some time ago at the Dutch Gallery, Hanover Square, pictures and studies of cats, which had a wonderful originality, and attracted the attention of many spectators, not much given to sentimentality.

But perhaps the greatest devotion that has ever drawn forth by the cat was that which Gotfried Mind, who was called the "Katzen-rafael" (the "Cat Raphael"), expended upon his pictures of it. Few of my readers can have heard of this artist, for he lived a very obscure life, and the admirable quality of his work hardly attracted any notice after his death. There is something peculiarly pathetic in his short biography. He was a most notable example of genius depressed, but never extinguished, by unusually unfavourable circumstances. From a short notice of his life, illustrated by ten plates of cat-groups from his pencil, published at Leipsic upwards of seventy years ago, we learn that he was born at Berne in 1768. At school he could not be taught the simplest elements of knowledge; he had great difficulty in writing his own name, and his mind always remained at the lowest grade. But he early developed an extraordinary talent for representing cats, and through his whole life he applied himself to his one task with the most absorbing zeal. With all cats he struck up a most remarkable friendship, which conquered their natural reserve, and made them devoted to him. While painting, a cat always sat on his back or shoulder, and he would keep for hours the most awkward postures so as not to disturb it. Frequently there was a second cat sitting on the table beside him, watching how the work went on; sometimes a kitten or two lay in his lap under the table. With these cats he kept up a playful, loving style of conversation; while if any human being interrupted him at such times he was greeted with frowns and growls. He had the art to seize the general nature of the animal, and in his portraits of their various physiognomies he delineated with the utmost truthfulness the specific character of each. To all his pictures he imparted a peculiar charm by a happy imitation of the soft velvety fur of the cat.'

Gottfried Mind drawing. Image courtesy of thegreatcat.org

Gottfried Mind drawing. Note the kitten's interest in the bees.

Having serendipitously (a splendid word) stumbled across Rev. Macmillan's article, I began to search for other references to famous men, particularly those in the field of literature, who were cat-lovers. Although I was familiar with the title, having encountered it somewhere in the distant past, *The Tiger in the House* (New York: Knopf, 1920) by Carl Van Vechten was otherwise a book of which I knew nothing. On randomly delving into its pages, by uncanny coincidence, the first thing I read was an account of Gottfried Mind:

> 'The painter and his cats were inseparable and his Minette was always by his side. Sometimes she would sit upon his knees while kittens perched on his shoulders and rather than disturb his friends he would remain in one attitude for hours.'

Minette! I could hardly believe it. And not only did his faithful cat have the same name as my first, but the artist

MINETTE WASHES
From a drawing by Gottfried Mind

also had cats sit on his shoulders and was reluctant to move for hours so as not to disturb those that had settled on him. There were certainly parallels between us, although I do claim the ability to write my own name.

Van Vechten dedicated a whole chapter of his book to 'Literary Men Who Have Loved Cats', and he had this to say about the relationship between cat and author:

> 'As an inspiration to the author I do not think the cat can be over-estimated. He suggests so much grace, power, beauty, motion, mysticism. The perfect symmetry of his body urges one to achieve an equally perfect form. His colour and his line alone would serve to give any imaginative creator material for several pages of nervous description; on any subject, mind you, not necessarily on the cat himself. As for his intelligence, his occult power, they are so remarkable that I sometimes feel convinced that true cat-lover authors are indebted even more deeply than they believe to "cats of ebony, cats of flame" for their books. The sharp, but concealed claws, the contracting pupil of the eye, which allows only the necessary amount of light to enter, the independence, should be the best of models for any critic; the graceful movements of the animal who waves a glorious banner as he walks silently should stir the soul of any poet. The cat symbolizes, indeed, all that a good writer tries to put into his work. I do not wonder that some writers love cats; I am only surprised that all writers do not love cats.'

Many of the authors he goes on to mention are unlikely to be familiar to the modern reader, but everyone should know of Charles Dickens, the most popular English

Charles Dickens

Mark Twain, another literary cat-lover

novelist of his day, and perhaps of all time. Dickens was a cat-lover and Van Vechten relates, 'There is a familiar story about Dickens and a kitten first called William, but later, for good reasons, Williamina, who to attract the author's attention, persisted in putting out a candle by which he was reading.' On the death of another cat, Bob, who was deaf, Dickens was so grief-stricken that he had one of Bob's paws stuffed and put on an ivory blade with the engraved inscription 'C.D. In Memory of Bob 1862.' He used it as a letter opener so that Bob was never far from his thoughts. Dickens was reputed to have said, 'What greater gift than the love of a cat'.

Another author that Van Vechten mentions in relation to the love of cats is George Borrow (1803–1881). Although not a household name now, he had big success in his day with the novels *The Bible in Spain*, *Lavengro*, *Romany Rye* and *Wild Wales*.

> 'When he [Borrow] went for a walk the dogs and the cat would set out with him, but the cat would turn back after accompanying him for about a quarter of a mile. When a favourite cat was so ill that he crawled away to die in solitude, Borrow went in search of him, and discovering the poor creature in the garden-hedge, carried him back into the house, laid him in a comfortable place, and watched over him until he died.'

Once again, here we have a touching reference to a cat finding a secluded spot in which to die, and I can fully understand how Borrow felt when he sought it out and brought it back into the house.

On the subject of grief for a departed cat, Van Vechten quotes from the French novelist Huysmans, '"In the matter of animals I love only cats but I love them unreasonably for their qualities and in spite of their numerous faults. I have only one but I could not live without a cat." But later he wrote, "I have been and still am a diligent friend of the feline race, but since the death of my last cat I do not own one; my affection is then for the present entirely platonic." This feeling that there will never be another, after the death of a cat, is pretty generally distributed, but in time another usually comes.'

Another literary giant that Van Vechten identified as being fond of cats is the American author Edgar Allan Poe, of whom he wrote:

> '"The Black Cat" is perhaps not the story of a cat-lover; nevertheless Poe loved cats, and there are those who even assert that Baudelaire inherited this passion from Poe, and took it over together with the other paraphernalia of the alchemist's retreat. At any rate a visitor to Poe in Fordham in 1846, describes this scene in his cottage: "There was no clothing on the bed, which was only straw, but a snow-white counterpane and sheets. The weather was cold and the sick lady (Mrs. Poe) had the dreadful chills that accompany the hectic fever of consumption. She lay on the straw bed, wrapped in her husband's great coat, with a large tortoiseshell cat in her bosom. The wonderful cat seemed conscious of her great usefulness. The coat and the cat were the sufferer's only means of warmth, except as her husband held her hands and her mother her feet."'

The above is a mere selection of the cat-loving authors

referred to in Carl Van Vechten's well-researched and well-written book, which is unbelievably almost a century old now. Below is one last quotation from his work, relating to Samuel Langhorne Clemens, better known to us as Mark Twain, the author of *Huckleberry Finn*.

> 'Mark Twain completely capitulated to grimalkin; cats, indeed, it would seem were one of the necessities of life to him. In "Pudd'nhead Wilson" he says, "A home without a cat, and a well-fed, well-petted, and properly revered cat, may be a perfect home, *perhaps*, but how can it prove its title?" Cat comparisons, cat allusions, cat descriptions, cat figures, cats and kittens abound in his stories.'

Twain, of course, is renowned for his witty epigrams and is among the most quoted men in history. From *Pudd'nhead Wilson* comes the incisively humorous quip, 'One of the most striking differences between a cat and a lie is that a cat has only nine lives.' Another of his cat-related observations is, 'Of all God's creatures there is only one that cannot be made the slave of the lash. That one is the cat. If man could be crossed with the cat it would improve man, but it would deteriorate the cat.' (*Notebook*, 1894).

In more recent times, Ernest Hemingway, William S. Burroughs, Jack Kerouac, Raymond Chandler, Philip K. Dick and Stephen King are noted among America authors as being cat men, although it is T. S. Eliot whose name has come to be most associated with cats. His book of light verse, *Old Possum's Book of Practical Cats*, became the inspiration for the highly successful musical *Cats* by Andrew Lloyd Weber. However, many readers today are perhaps unaware of Paul Gallico whose most successful books were probably *The Poseidon Adventure* and *The Snow Goose*—a rather moving novella concerning the evacuation from Dunkirk in 1940. Everyone ought to read *The Snow Goose*. In 1964 Gallico produced *The Silent Miaow*, although the book was ostensibly written in original feline by a cat as a guide to captivating and controlling humans. It was profusely illustrated with photographs by Suzanne Szasz and 'translated' by Gallico. It remains a cat classic and a copy is still in my collection today.

www.ingramcontent.com/pod-product-compliance
Lightning Source LLC
Chambersburg PA
CBHW060444040426
42331CB00044B/2599